Shortcut Cooking For The Holidays

Great American Opportunities, Inc./ Favorite Recipes® Press

President: Thomas F. McDow III
Editorial Manager: Mary Jane Blount
Editors: Georgia Brazil, Mary Cummings,
Jane Hinshaw, Linda Jones, Mary Wilson
Typography: Jessie Anglin, Sara Anglin,
Pam Newsome

This cookbook is a collection of our favorite recipes which are not necessarily original recipes.

Published by: Favorite Recipes® Press, a division of
Great American Opportunities, Inc.
P.O. Box 305142
Nashville, Tennessee 37230

Manufactured in the United States of America
First Printing: 1993   25,000 copies

All-American Holidays

Americans love holidays and celebrate for almost any reason: religious ceremonies, uniquely American happenings, personal family traditions. We honor our heroes, our parents and grandparents, our bosses and secretaries. We make happenings of the first snowfall or of a raise, kindergarten graduations and even paying taxes.

If we chart our holidays, we find a progression through the months which suggests that not only do we love to celebrate, we also want a steady stream of events to mark our calendars. We invented Super Bowl Sunday for January and Thanksgiving Day for November with all kinds of holidays in between.

Our melting-pot culture has assimilated ideas for every season from around the world. In March, everyone is Irish and wears green although such celebrations do not take place in Ireland. Pumpkins grin or scowl in October; bunnies lay chocolate eggs in the spring; and reindeer fly in December. We celebrate occasions as diverse as Earth Day, Hanukkah and Ground Hog Day. We find reasons to celebrate: graduations, weddings, anniversaries, falling leaves, new homes, retirement and even straight "A's."

From the first day of the year to the last day of the year, each month brings both traditional holidays and new opportunities for making any day special. The common thread that connects all our joyous, happy days is the memories of warmth and sharing, which are, after all, the real reasons we love to celebrate.

Nutritional Guidelines

The editors have attempted to present these family recipes in a form that allows approximate nutritional values to be computed. Persons with dietary or health problems or whose diets require close monitoring should not rely solely on the nutritional information provided. They should consult their physicians or a registered dietitian for specific information.

Abbreviations for Nutritional Analysis

Cal — Calories
Prot — Protein
Carbo — Carbohydrates

Dietary Fiber — Fiber
T Fat — Total Fat
Chol — Cholesterol

Sod — Sodium
gr — gram
mg — milligrams

Nutritional information for these recipes is computed from information derived from many sources, including materials supplied by the United States Department of Agriculture, computer databanks and journals in which the information is assumed to be in the public domain. However, many specialty items, new products and processed foods may not be available from these sources or may vary from the average values used in these analyses. More information on new and/or specific products may be obtained by reading the nutrient labels. Unless otherwise specified, the nutritional analysis of these recipes is based on all measurements being level.

- **Artificial sweeteners** vary in use and strength so should be used "to taste," using the recipe ingredients as a guideline. Sweeteners using aspartame (NutraSweet and Equal) should not be used as a sweetener in recipes involving prolonged heating which reduces the sweet taste. For further information, refer to package information.
- **Alcoholic ingredients** have been analyzed for the basic ingredients, although cooking evaporates the alcohol thus decreasing caloric content.
- **Buttermilk, sour cream** and **yogurt** are the types available commercially.
- **Cake mixes** which are prepared using package directions include 3 eggs and ½ cup oil.
- **Chicken**, cooked for boning and chopping, has been roasted; this method yields the lowest caloric values.
- **Cottage cheese** is cream-style with 4.2% creaming mixture. Dry-curd cottage cheese has no creaming mixture.
- **Eggs** are all large. (To avoid raw eggs that may carry salmonella as in eggnog or 6-week muffin batter, use an equivalent amount of commercial egg substitute.)
- **Flour** is unsifted all-purpose flour.
- **Garnishes**, serving suggestions and other optional additions and variations are not included in the analysis.
- **Margarine** and **butter** are regular, not whipped or presoftened.
- **Milk** is whole milk, 3.5% butterfat. Lowfat milk is 1% butterfat. Evaporated milk is whole milk with 60% of the water removed.
- **Oil** is any type of vegetable cooking oil. Shortening is hydrogenated vegetable shortening.
- **Salt** and other ingredients to taste as noted in the ingredients have not been included in the nutritional analysis.
- If a choice of ingredients has been given, the analysis reflects the first option. If a choice of amounts has been given, the analysis reflects the greater amount.

Table of Contents

Celebrating the Easy, Earth-Friendly Way

Whether you think the three "R's" are what your grandmother learned in school... three letters in the words "PARTY! PARTY! PARTY!"... or the bywords of ecology: "Reduce"—"Reuse"—"Recycle"... you're right. So, **Read** these pages, **'Rite** your notes, and do your **'Rithmatic: Reducing** what we buy, **Reusing** what we have, and **Recycling** what we can not only gives the Earth something to celebrate, but makes our own parties easy and special at the same time.

Decorating—Naturally

Some of the most beautiful—and the easiest—decorations can literally be found in your own backyard. Start with what's in season: tulips, daffodils, iris or flowering branches in spring; Queen Anne's lace, roses, marigolds and zinnias in summer; cattails, bittersweet, autumn leaves, and chrysanthemums in fall; pine boughs, holly, amaryllis and forced bulbs in winter. Whatever the season, bring it indoors and celebrate!

If your backyard is a balcony, you can decorate from your favorite "grocery" garden. Asparagus stalks tied with ribbon or a mountain of strawberries bring spring indoors. Cherry tomato plants or beautiful cabbages and red bell peppers are colorful summer delights. Pumpkins, gourds, apples and artichokes put on a vibrant fall show. Dried potpourri, cinnamon sticks and citrus fruits are winter tantalizers.

Arrange the plants and flowers in vases, bowls, pitchers, casseroles, or in mason jars; heap vegetables and fruit in baskets or on trays; serve dips, soups and vegetables in hollowed out cabbages, pumpkins, peppers and squash. Plants and flowers can be composted and the fruits and vegetables used in holiday cooking. Decorations using nature's bounty are easy, beautiful, economical and ecological.

Season to Season

Every season and holiday has its charms, and with the use of natural decorations available, we can match our surroundings to Nature's. Just because the seasons change, however, decorating doesn't have to be difficult. The same elements used in winter can be charming in summer—or any other time. With a little magic, you can always be ready for a holiday celebration.

One lady we know works her magic with a grapevine wreath. Hers is on her front door, but yours could be over the fireplace, on the dining room table, in the kitchen, or even in a bedroom. In January, the wreath is sprinkled with glittery snowflakes. Snowflakes are followed by hearts, shamrocks, colored eggs, May baskets, summer flowers, tiny flags, goblins and harvest fruits in turn. A birch branch anchored in a decorative pot indoors or a suitable shrub outdoors could easily serve the same function changing from a Valentine tree, a birthday tree or a Halloween tree as the occasion arises.

Baskets used as centerpieces, hearth decorations, or bookcase toppers can likewise hold a changing parade of appropriate fillers: daisies, fall leaves, evergreen branches, flags, pine cones, apples, flowering plants, balloons and stuffed animals. Or, fill the basket with an arrangement to match your decor and make a slipcover for the basket itself using fabric with seasonal motifs. Add a small decoration or two for specific holidays, and you're ready to go.

The Celebration Closet

Whatever reusable decorations you choose, you'll need a way to organize them and your other party essentials. Set aside a trunk, hamper, drawer or closet to hold the accessories you'll use over and over again in countless ways to create festive occasions.

Stash a selection of tablecloths, place mats and napkins in red, white, green and blue. By mixing and matching, you can create a table setting for Valentine's Day, Earth Day, or Independence Day, just to name a few possibilities. Keep an assortment of matching candles and napkin rings as well as a collection of various size vases, baskets and candle holders. When a holiday comes your way, you'll be ready without spending a bundle of money for paper accessories.

The Perfect Gift

Lots of holidays call for gifts, and even those that don't are made more special with a small memento. We give to our mothers and dads on their days, to sweethearts on Valentine's Day, to the planet on Earth Day, to secret friends on May Day. Some of our most treasured gifts (like tiny hand prints in plaster or finger-painted originals) will never appear on the shopper's network or in a fancy store. What makes them—and all handmade gifts— special is the love and care that goes into their making.

Craft books and magazines are filled with gift ideas that make picking a perfect present for any person and any occasion a cinch. A chef's apron decorated with children's hand prints is a great gift for moms, dads and grandparents. Squares of an old quilt made into pillows or framed as art will bring joy to all who remember the original. A collage of bits and pieces of memorabilia in a shadow box frame can be tailored exactly for the lucky recipient.

The pages of *Shortcut Cooking for the Holidays* are filled with delicious recipes that make great gifts as well. Cakes, breads, munchies and candy—all easy and all sure to be appreciated. Mix and match recipes to suit the occasion. Make a green pie for a friend on St. Patrick's Day, or decorate a white dessert with blueberries and strawberries for a Fourth of July present. Best of all, any gift you make gives pleasure twice—to the fortunate person who receives it and to the thoughtful giver.

Wrapping It Up

While homemade gifts tend to follow the three ecological "R's" by reducing waste, reusing and recycling, it's in the wrapping that we can be even more caring. Wrap children's gifts in recycled funny papers, or make your own wrap by sponge printing recycled brown paper. Use decorated lunch bags to hold baked goodies. Wrap loaves of bread in reusable fabric. Present baked goods in muffin, cake or bread pans for reusable containers. Buy one-of-a-kind plates at tag or garage sales to hold cakes and cookies. Package assorted small presents in mugs, pitchers, baskets or even flowerpots. These cost no more than fancy gift wraps and make two gifts out of one.

Menus for All Seasons

All the recipes in *Shortcut Cooking for the Holidays* are delicious enough for any celebration and easy and nutritious enough for any day. Mix and match to suit your style: an all-green dinner for Irish luck; hearty soups and nibbles for a football tailgate; a table of desserts for a sweet Valentine's Day party. We've included some super samples on the following pages to get you going. Use your imagination and our recipes!

Above all, take the time to find special pleasure in each day, each season. Look for holidays to remember. Create your own special days. Celebrate life and each other!

Super Bowl Snack-a-Thon

The very nature of this occasion is informal, and if the cook plans ahead with these easy recipes, he or she can put her feet up and enjoy it with the rest of the couch potatoes.

Melting Pot Munch   Chili Cheesers
Cajun Shrimp   Fruited Cocktail Weiners
Salsa Mushrooms or Spinach-Pita Appetizers
Zesty Breadsticks
Popcorn Cake and Brownie Bites

Sweetheart Dinner for Two

Our special dinner would be perfect for your Valentine or for an anniversary tête-à-tête at any season of the year.

Apple Cider-Onion Soup   Scallops and Pasta
Gingered Asparagus   Herbed Bread
Luscious Lemon Cream and Fruit
White Grape Juice Sparkler

St. Patrick's Day Supper

To keep it simple and make it fun, try these recipes for a casual green supper.

Spinach and Leek Dip   Cream of Asparagus Soup
Heavenly Pistachio Salad
Cheesy Ham and Broccoli Bread
Mint and Fudge Cake   Lime Coolers

Hard Times Party

Plan this get-together to console yourself and your friends after such traumas as satisfying the Internal Revenue Service. It features CCC, or Cheap Comfort for Crisis.

Souper Cheddar Dip
Speedy White Chili   Coleslaw
Corn Bread   Butterfinger Crunch   Root Beer

(See Index for Recipes)

Derby Day Fling

Our menu would be just as appropriate for May Day or Ground Hog Day or for any other occasion which offers an excuse for an easy celebration.

Golden Glow Punch   Herbed Cheese Balls
Molded Gazpacho Salad   Chicken Lasagna
Bubble Loaves   Easy Fruity Crown Cake

Mother's Day Luncheon

An elegant menu which is simple enough for even a rookie cook to prepare would serve as well for Father's Day or Grandparent's Day.

Fruit Compote   Mustard-Baked Chicken
Broccoli with Almonds   Herbed Rice
Yogurt Muffins   Quick Peach Melba
Iced Tea

Graduation Dinner

This simply elegant dinner will make a special occasion of most any celebratory occasion.

Baked Brie Rounds   Citrus Green Salad
Steak Bonne Femme or Teriyaki Flank Steak
Tomato-Basil Fettucini
Strawberry Parfait Pie   Mock Champagne

Fourth of July Barbecue

A change from the usual hamburger cookout—this is the perfect casual meal to enjoy on the deck with family and friends of all ages.

Artichoke Chili Dip   Chips
Gingered Fruit Cup
Beef Fajitas   Tortillas
Spanish Bean Casserole
Freezer Ice Cream   Cookies
Soft Drinks   Iced Tea

(See Index for Recipes)

Homecoming Reunion Buffet

Yours may be a family reunion or a football weekend college reunion, but your guests will enjoy this menu for either occasion.

Shrimp Louis Dip   Vegetables   Crackers
Molded Ambrosia   Peppered Beef Tenderloin Roast
Zippy Broccoli   Honey-Baked Onions
Easy Herb Bread   Fruit Stand Pie   Apple Spice Spritzer

Monster Meal

Holidays should always include the children and this menu would be suitable for a birthday or for that special holiday of childhood—Halloween.

Taco Pizza Dip   Chips   Bread Rounds
Healthy Heavenly Hash   Vienna Burgers   Baked Potato Fans
Easy Popcorn Balls   Iced Pretzels
Apple-Pineapple Punch

Holiday Family Dinner

Celebrate any traditional holiday with our heavily laden board.

Pumpkin Soup   Holiday Ribbon Salad
Roast Turkey   San Francisco Stuffing
Lemony Green Beans
Sweet Potatoes in Apple Shells
Fresh Cranberry Relish   Hot Rolls
Instant Boiled Custard   Holiday Charlotte

End-of-the-Year Dinner

This menu offers an easy way to celebrate, recycling some of the leftovers in the refrigerator and giving them an entirely new twist.

Easy Peanut Soup   Exotic Curried Turkey
Romaine Salad   Cheddar-Garlic Bread
Eggnogging Chocolate Cake

(See Index for Recipes)

Great Beginnings

Celebrations call for a special array of knock-out goodies but present a holiday dilemma: how to serve great food that doesn't sabotage our guests' (and our own) diets. Here, you'll find terrific finger foods to indulge in without a moment's guilt and there are fabulous easy recipes for delicious soups and salads as well. Serve as separate courses for a festive start to special dinners. And, plan great parties around the foods in just this section—a hearty soup supper to celebrate the first snowfall or an all-appetizer open house to usher in the holidays. With foods like these, your table itself will be cause enough for celebrating.

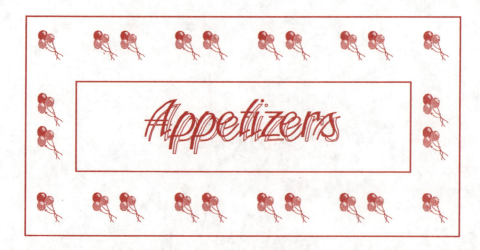

Appetizers

Artichoke Chili Dip

1 4-ounce can chopped green
  chilies
1 cup grated Parmesan cheese
1 14-ounce can artichoke hearts,
  drained

1 cup light mayonnaise
6 to 12 drops of hot sauce, or to
  taste
1 12-ounce package tortilla
  chips

Preheat oven to 350 degrees. Combine undrained chilies, cheese, artichokes and mayonnaise in bowl; mix well. Spoon into lightly greased 1-quart baking dish. Bake for 15 to 20 minutes or until heated through. Sprinkle with hot sauce. Serve with chips. Yield: 6 servings.

Approx Per Serving: Cal 461; Prot 11 g; Carbo 44 g; Fiber 2 g;
    T Fat 28 g; 53% Calories from Fat; Chol 21 mg; Sod 1031 mg.

Souper Cheddar Dip

1 10-ounce can Cheddar cheese
  soup
1 cup shredded sharp Cheddar
  cheese
1/2 teaspoon dry mustard

1 8 1/2-ounce container French
  onion dip
Pepper to taste
1 16-ounce loaf French bread

Combine soup, cheese, mustard, dip and pepper in saucepan; mix well. Cook until cheese is melted, stirring frequently. Pour into fondue pot. Cut French bread into bite-sized pieces. Serve with dip. Yield: 8 servings.

Approx Per Serving: Cal 337; Prot 12 g; Carbo 36 g; Fiber 1 g;
    T Fat 15 g; 41% Calories from Fat; Chol 23 mg; Sod 982 mg.

Roasted Corn and Avocado Dip

1 cup frozen whole kernel corn, thawed
2 teaspoons oil
2 large avocados
1 medium tomato, finely chopped
2 tablespoons minced onion
2 cloves of garlic, minced
1 2-ounce can jalapeño peppers, chopped
3 tablespoons lime juice
1/4 teaspoon cumin
1/2 teaspoon salt
8 tomato wedges
1 8-ounce package each yellow and blue cornmeal chips

Preheat oven to 400 degrees. Combine corn and oil in shallow baking dish; mix well. Bake for 8 minutes or until light brown, stirring twice. Set aside to cool. Chop 1 avocado. Mash remaining avocado in bowl. Add chopped avocado, corn, chopped tomato, onion, garlic, jalapeño peppers, lime juice, cumin and salt; mix gently. Chill, covered, for up to 24 hours. Spoon into serving bowl. Garnish with tomato wedges. Serve with chips for dipping. Yield: 8 servings.

Approx Per Serving: Cal 400; Prot 7 g; Carbo 45 g; Fiber 9 g; T Fat 24 g; 51% Calories from Fat; Chol 0 mg; Sod 527 mg.

Polynesian Crab Dip

1 7-ounce can crab meat, drained
1 cup coconut
1 cup light mayonnaise-type salad dressing
1 cup light sour cream
1/4 cup chopped onion
1/4 teaspoon curry powder
2 tablespoons chopped parsley
1 2-ounce can sliced mushrooms, drained

Mix all ingredients in bowl. Chill until serving time. Yield: 12 servings.

Approx Per Serving: Cal 120; Prot 4 g; Carbo 7 g; Fiber 1 g; T Fat 9 g; 63% Calories from Fat; Chol 28 mg; Sod 184 mg.

Roasted Pepper Dip

1 5-ounce jar roasted red peppers, drained, finely chopped
1 4-ounce can chopped green chilies, drained
1 cup light sour cream
1 cup light mayonnaise
1 tablespoon lemon juice
1/2 teaspoon garlic powder
3 cups bite-sized fresh vegetables

Mix first 6 ingredients in bowl. Spoon into serving bowl. Chill until serving time. Serve with vegetables for dipping. Yield: 8 servings.

Approx Per Serving: Cal 128; Prot 2 g; Carbo 9 g; Fiber 1 g; T Fat 10 g; 67% Calories from Fat; Chol 20 mg; Sod 283 mg.

Shrimp Louis Dip

1 cup light mayonnaise
1 cup light sour cream
1/4 cup chili sauce
1 tablespoon prepared
   horseradish
1/4 teaspoon salt

1/8 teaspoon pepper
1/3 cup finely chopped green bell
   pepper
2 cups finely chopped cooked
   shrimp

Combine first 6 ingredients in bowl; mix well. Fold in green pepper and shrimp. Spoon into serving dish. Chill until serving time. Serve with chips and vegetables. Yield: 16 servings.

Approx Per Serving: Cal 81; Prot 5 g; Carbo 4 g; Fiber <1 g;
   T Fat 5 g; 56% Calories from Fat; Chol 52 mg; Sod 220 mg.

Spinach and Leek Dip

1 10-ounce package frozen
   chopped spinach, thawed
1 1/2 cups light sour cream
1 cup light mayonnaise
1 envelope Swiss leek soup mix
1 bunch green onions, chopped

1 8-ounce can sliced water
   chestnuts, drained, chopped
1/4 teaspoon Dijon mustard
5 drops of Tabasco sauce
1 16-ounce loaf sourdough
   bread

Squeeze excess moisture from spinach. Combine with next 7 ingredients in bowl; mix well. Chill for 2 hours. Cut top from bread. Hollow out center, leaving 1/2-inch shell. Cut center and top into cubes. Spoon dip into bread. Serve with bread cubes or crackers and vegetables. Yield: 8 servings.

Approx Per Serving: Cal 333; Prot 10 g; Carbo 44 g; Fiber 2 g;
   T Fat 14 g; 37% Calories from Fat; Chol 27 mg; Sod 878 mg.

Taco Pizza Dip

16 ounces light cream cheese,
   softened
2 envelopes taco seasoning mix
1 cup plain nonfat yogurt,
   drained
2 tomatoes, chopped

1/2 head lettuce, shredded
2 or 3 green onions, chopped
2 cups shredded Cheddar cheese
16 ounces toasted Italian bread
   rounds

Combine cream cheese, taco seasoning mix and yogurt in bowl; mix well. Spread in pizza pan. Top with tomatoes, lettuce, green onions and Cheddar cheese. Serve with bread rounds. Yield: 20 servings.

Approx Per Serving: Cal 184; Prot 8 g; Carbo 19 g; Fiber 1 g;
   T Fat 8 g; 39% Calories from Fat; Chol 25 mg; Sod 692 mg.

Herbed Cheese Balls

16 ounces light cream cheese,
  softened
1 tablespoon milk
2 teaspoons chicken-flavored
  instant bouillon

1/2 teaspoon each basil leaves,
  marjoram leaves, oregano
  leaves and thyme leaves
1/4 teaspoon garlic powder
Cracked black pepper to taste

Combine cream cheese and milk in mixer bowl; beat until smooth and creamy. Add bouillon, herbs and garlic powder; mix well. Chill for 1 hour or until firm enough to shape. Divide into 2 portions. Shape each portion into ball; roll in cracked pepper to coat. Wrap in plastic wrap. Chill for 3 hours or until firm. Yield: 8 servings.

Approx Per Serving: Cal 129; Prot 6 g; Carbo 4 g; Fiber 0 g;
  T Fat 10 g; 68% Calories from Fat; Chol 33 mg; Sod 613 mg.

Quick-and-Easy Cheese Ball

16 ounces light cream cheese,
  softened
2 tablespoons chopped green
  olives
1 cup small curd low-fat cottage
  cheese

2 teaspoons grated onion
2 teaspoons Worcestershire sauce
3 or 4 dashes of hot sauce
12 ounces dried beef, finely
  chopped

Mix first 6 ingredients in bowl. Add half the beef; mix well. Shape into ball; chill. Roll in remaining beef. Serve with crackers. Yield: 8 servings.

Approx Per Serving: Cal 226; Prot 22 g; Carbo 6 g; Fiber <1 g;
  T Fat 12 g; 50% Calories from Fat; Chol 104 mg; Sod 1988 mg.

Curried Chicken Spread

16 ounces light cream cheese,
  softened
2 cups low-fat cottage cheese
1/2 cup light sour cream
4 teaspoons curry powder
1   10-ounce jar chutney

2/3 cup chopped green onions
2/3 cup raisins
2/3 cup flaked coconut
2 cups chopped cooked chicken
1 cup chopped salted peanuts
1/4 cup chopped green onions

Combine first 4 ingredients in bowl; beat well. Spread in 9x13-inch dish. Spoon chutney over top. Sprinkle with mixture of 2/3 cup green onions, raisins and coconut. Top with chicken. Garnish with chopped peanuts and 1/4 cup green onions. Serve with crackers. Yield: 8 servings.

Approx Per Serving: Cal 457; Prot 29 g; Carbo 32 g; Fiber 4 g;
  T Fat 25 g; 48% Calories from Fat; Chol 74 mg; Sod 862 mg.

Deviled Egg Spread

1 medium onion, chopped
3 stalks celery, chopped
6 hard-cooked eggs, chopped
1   3-ounce package lemon gelatin
1/2 cup boiling water
16 ounces light cream cheese,
     softened

1 teaspoon prepared mustard
1/2 teaspoon salt
1/2 teaspoon white pepper
1/8 teaspoon Tabasco sauce
3 tablespoons light mayonnaise

Process onion, celery and eggs separately in food processor container until very finely chopped. Combine in bowl. Dissolve gelatin in boiling water in bowl. Combine with cream cheese in food processor container. Process until smooth. Add mustard and seasonings. Process until blended. Add cream cheese mixture and mayonnaise to egg mixture; mix well. Pour into oiled 7-cup mold. Chill until set. Unmold onto serving plate. Serve with crackers. Yield: 8 servings.

Approx Per Serving: Cal 247; Prot 12 g; Carbo 16 g; Fiber 1 g;
     T Fat 15 g; 54% Calories from Fat; Chol 194 mg; Sod 590 mg.

Smoked Turkey Spread

1 pound smoked turkey
1/3 cup coarsely chopped celery
8 ounces soft cream cheese with
     chives and onion
1/4 cup milk
Spicy mustard to taste

Pepper to taste
1/2   10-ounce package frozen
     chopped spinach, thawed,
     drained
1 tablespoon lemon juice
1/4 cup toasted sliced almonds

Line 4-cup mold with plastic wrap. Chop turkey and celery in food processor container. Combine with half the cream cheese, milk, mustard and pepper in bowl; mix well. Combine spinach, lemon juice and remaining cream cheese in bowl; mix well. Layer half the turkey mixture, all the spinach mixture and remaining turkey mixture in prepared mold. Chill, covered, for several hours. Unmold onto serving plate. Sprinkle with almonds. Serve with assorted flatbreads. Yield 16 servings.

Approx Per Serving: Cal 99; Prot 8 g; Carbo 2 g; Fiber <1 g;
     T Fat 7 g; 62% Calories from Fat; Chol 29 mg; Sod 261 mg.

Serve your favorite dip in a hollowed-out round loaf of bread, a lettuce or cabbage, or in pepper cups or melon boats.

Apple Pie Sausage Balls

1 pound sausage
2 cups baking mix
1 cup raisins, chopped

1 cup grated apple
1/2 cup chopped walnuts
1/2 teaspoon apple pie spice

Preheat oven to 350 degrees. Combine sausage, baking mix, raisins, grated apple, walnuts and apple pie spice in bowl; mix well. Shape into 1-inch balls; place on baking sheet. Bake for 20 minutes or until light brown. Yield: 12 servings.

Approx Per Serving: Cal 242; Prot 6 g; Carbo 29 g; Fiber 2 g;
T Fat 12 g; 43% Calories from Fat; Chol 15 mg; Sod 496 mg.

Baked Brie Rounds

2 sourdough French rolls
1/2 cup margarine, softened
1/4 cup chopped almonds

1/2 cup packed light brown sugar
15 ounces Brie, cut into thin
wedges

Preheat oven to 375 degrees. Cut French rolls into 1/2-inch slices, discarding end rounds. Spread 1 side of slices with margarine. Combine almonds and brown sugar in bowl; mix well. Spread half the almond mixture on slices. Top with wedge of Brie and remaining almond mixture. Arrange on baking sheet. Bake for 6 to 7 minutes or until heated through. Yield: 12 servings.

Approx Per Serving: Cal 277; Prot 9 g; Carbo 19 g; Fiber <1 g;
T Fat 19 g; 61% Calories from Fat; Chol 35 mg; Sod 384 mg.

Brie with Almonds

1   15-ounce round Brie
1/4 cup honey-mustard
1/2 cup sliced almonds, toasted
2 red unpeeled apples, cut into
wedges

2 green unpeeled apples, cut into
wedges
1   6-ounce can pineapple juice

Remove rind from top of cheese, leaving 1/2-inch border. Place on large serving tray. Spread honey-mustard over top of cheese; sprinkle with almonds. Let stand at room temperature for 1 hour or longer. Toss apple wedges with pineapple juice in bowl; drain. Arrange on tray around cheese. Serve immediately. Yield 10 servings.

Approx Per Serving: Cal 223; Prot 10 g; Carbo 15 g; Fiber 2 g;
T Fat 15 g; 57% Calories from Fat; Chol 42 mg; Sod 320 mg.

Broccoli Bits

2   10-ounce packages frozen
    chopped broccoli, thawed,
    drained
2 tablespoons minced onion
3/4 cup shredded mozzarella
    cheese
3/4 cup grated Parmesan cheese

2 egg whites, beaten
1 teaspoon garlic powder
1 teaspoon thyme
1/2 cup melted margarine
2 1/2 cups fresh bread crumbs
1/2 cup seasoned Italian bread
    crumbs

Preheat oven to 350 degrees. Combine broccoli, onion, mozzarella cheese, Parmesan cheese, egg whites, garlic powder and thyme in bowl; mix well. Add margarine and 2 1/2 cups bread crumbs; mix well. Mixture will be very moist. Shape into 1-inch balls. Coat with 1/2 cup seasoned bread crumbs. Place 1 inch apart on baking sheet. Bake for 25 minutes. Yield: 24 servings.

Approx Per Serving: Cal 84; Prot 3 g; Carbo 5 g; Fiber 1 g;
    T Fat 6 g; 59% Calories from Fat; Chol 5 mg; Sod 154 mg.

Cheese Puffs

6 ounces light cream cheese
2 1/2 cups shredded Cheddar cheese
1 cup margarine

4 egg whites, stiffly beaten
1   16-ounce loaf white bread,
    crusts trimmed

Melt first 3 ingredients in double boiler, stirring occasionally. Fold in egg whites. Cut bread into cubes. Dip bread cubes into egg white mixture. Place on ungreased baking sheet. Chill overnight. Preheat oven to 375 degrees. Bake puffs for 10 to 15 minutes or until golden brown. Yield: 20 servings.

Approx Per Serving: Cal 220; Prot 7 g; Carbo 12 g; Fiber <1 g;
    T Fat 16 g; 66% Calories from Fat; Chol 20 mg; Sod 368 mg.

Chili Cheesers

8 eggs, beaten
1/2 cup all-purpose flour
1 teaspoon baking powder
3/4 teaspoon salt
1 1/2 cups low-fat cottage cheese

3 cups shredded Monterey Jack
    cheese
2   4-ounce cans green chilies,
    drained, seeded, chopped

Preheat oven to 350 degrees. Beat eggs with flour, baking powder and salt in bowl. Add cottage cheese, Monterey Jack cheese and chilies; mix well. Spoon into greased 9x13-inch baking pan. Bake for 40 minutes. Let stand for 10 minutes. Cut into small squares to serve. Yield: 12 servings.

Approx Per Serving: Cal 208; Prot 16 g; Carbo 7 g; Fiber <1 g;
    T Fat 13 g; 56% Calories from Fat; Chol 170 mg; Sod 607 mg.

Crunchy Chicken Bites

1   5-ounce can chunk chicken
1/2 cup shredded cheese
1   8-ounce can water chestnuts,
    drained, chopped
1/4 cup light mayonnaise
2 tablespoons chopped onion

1 teaspoon lemon juice
1/4 teaspoon curry powder
Pepper to taste
1   8-ounce can flaky rolls
3 tablespoons chutney

Preheat oven to 350 degrees. Combine first 8 ingredients in bowl; mix well. Separate each roll into 3 portions. Arrange on baking sheet. Spread with chicken mixture and chutney. Bake for 10 minutes or until golden brown. Yield: 15 servings.

Approx Per Serving: Cal 96; Prot 4 g; Carbo 11 g; Fiber 1 g;
    T Fat 4 g; 37% Calories from Fat; Chol 6 mg; Sod 284 mg.

Sweet and Sour Chicken Nuggets

2 pounds chicken breast filets,
    cut into 1-inch pieces
Garlic salt to taste
1 egg
2 teaspoons water
1/2 cup cornstarch

2 tablespoons oil
1 1/2 cups sugar
3/4 cup white vinegar
1/3 cup catsup
2 tablespoons reduced-sodium
    soy sauce

Sprinkle chicken with garlic salt. Dip in mixture of egg and water. Coat with cornstarch. Brown in oil in skillet. Place in serving dish; keep warm. Combine sugar, vinegar, catsup and soy sauce in saucepan. Cook until thickened, stirring frequently. Pour over chicken. Yield: 8 servings.

Approx Per Serving: Cal 371; Prot 28 g; Carbo 49 g; Fiber <1 g;
    T Fat 7 g; 17% Calories from Fat; Chol 99 mg; Sod 384 mg.

Stuffed Endive Spears

1/2 cup part-skim ricotta cheese
2 tablespoons crumbled bleu
    cheese
Salt and red pepper to taste

2 heads endive, separated into
    spears
1/2 cup chopped walnuts, toasted

Combine ricotta cheese, bleu cheese, salt and red pepper in food processor container fitted with metal blade. Process for 15 seconds or until smooth. Spoon 1 teaspoon cheese mixture onto stem end of each endive spear; sprinkle with walnuts. Yield: 8 servings.

Approx Per Serving: Cal 84; Prot 4 g; Carbo 4 g; Fiber 1 g;
    T Fat 6 g; 65% Calories from Fat; Chol 6 mg; Sod 57 mg.

Miniature Ham-Filled Cream Puffs

1 cup water
1/2 cup margarine
1 cup all-purpose flour
4 eggs
3   41/2-ounce cans deviled ham

1 tablespoon prepared
   horseradish
3/4 teaspoon pepper
1/4 teaspoon onion salt
1/3 cup light sour cream

Preheat oven to 400 degrees. Bring water and margarine to a rolling boil in saucepan. Add flour. Cook over low heat until mixture forms ball, stirring constantly; remove from heat. Add eggs. Beat until smooth and glossy. Drop by rounded teaspoonfuls onto ungreased baking sheet. Bake for 20 minutes or until puffed and dry. Cool on wire rack. Combine ham, horseradish, seasonings and sour cream in bowl. Chill in refrigerator. Split puffs; remove soft centers. Fill with ham mixture. Arrange on serving plate. Yield: 20 servings.

Approx Per Serving: Cal 151; Prot 5 g; Carbo 5 g; Fiber <1 g;
    T Fat 12 g; 73% Calories from Fat; Chol 59 mg; Sod 325 mg.

Reuben Mushrooms

1/4 cup sauerkraut, rinsed,
   drained
1/4 cup shredded Swiss cheese
1   3-ounce package sliced
   corned beef, chopped

2 tablespoons rye cracker crumbs
2 tablespoons Thousand Island
   salad dressing
20 large fresh mushrooms

Combine sauerkraut, cheese, corned beef, cracker crumbs and salad dressing in bowl; mix well. Set aside. Clean mushrooms, discarding stems. Arrange 10 at a time around outer edge of 12-inch glass plate. Cover with vented plastic wrap. Microwave on High for 2 to 5 minutes or until almost tender, turning plate once. Invert onto paper towels to drain. Fill mushroom caps with corned beef mixture. Arrange 10 at a time around outer edge of plate. Microwave, uncovered, on High for 21/2 to 31/2 minutes or until mushrooms are heated through, turning plate once. Yield: 10 servings.

Approx Per Serving: Cal 53; Prot 4 g; Carbo 5 g; Fiber 1 g;
    T Fat 3 g; 42% Calories from Fat; Chol 3 mg; Sod 90 mg.

For a large party, arrange small attractive plates of appetizers, which can be refilled easily, rather than a large one which loses its attractiveness as guests enjoy it.

Salsa Mushrooms

2 pounds fresh large mushrooms
5 7-ounce cans green chili salsa
1 5-ounce jar pimento-stuffed
  olives

1 teaspoon salt
Chopped fresh cilantro or parsley
  to taste

Mix mushrooms with salsa, olives and salt in bowl. Marinate, covered, in refrigerator overnight. Sprinkle with cilantro. Yield: 12 servings.

Approx Per Serving: Cal 84; Prot 4 g; Carbo 14 g; Fiber 2 g;
    T Fat 6 g; 42% Calories from Fat; Chol 0 mg; Sod 1038 mg.

Olive Muffinettes

1 10-ounce package corn bread
  mix
1 egg, beaten

$1/2$ cup sour cream dip with
  chives
24 pimento-stuffed olives

Preheat oven to 400 degrees. Combine corn bread mix, egg and dip in bowl; mix well. Fill greased $13/4$-inch muffin cups $3/4$ full. Press olive into each cup. Bake for 15 minutes or until golden brown. Yield: 12 servings.

Approx Per Serving: Cal 83; Prot 2 g; Carbo 9 g; Fiber <1 g;
    T Fat 5 g; 49% Calories from Fat; Chol 22 mg; Sod 316 mg.

Olive Nips

$1/2$ cup all-purpose flour
$1/8$ teaspoon dry mustard
$1/4$ teaspoon salt
1 cup shredded sharp Cheddar
  cheese

1 teaspoon milk
2 to 3 tablespoons minced onion
3 tablespoons melted margarine
1 or 2 drops of Tabasco sauce
24 pimento-stuffed olives

Preheat oven to 400 degrees. Mix flour, dry mustard, salt and cheese in bowl. Add milk, onion, margarine and Tabasco sauce; mix well. Shape into balls around olives, covering completely. Place on baking sheet. Bake for 10 to 12 minutes or until golden brown. Yield: 8 servings.

Approx Per Serving: Cal 139; Prot 5 g; Carbo 7 g; Fiber 1 g;
    T Fat 11 g; 69% Calories from Fat; Chol 15 mg; Sod 486 mg.

Reuben Phyllo Rolls

4 ounces deli sliced corned beef
1/2 cup rinsed drained sauerkraut
4 ounces low sodium Swiss
cheese, shredded

1 tablespoon Dijon mustard
7 sheets frozen phyllo dough,
thawed
3 tablespoons oil

Preheat oven to 375 degrees. Combine corned beef, sauerkraut, cheese and mustard in bowl; mix well. Place 1 sheet phyllo dough on waxed paper, leaving remaining dough covered with damp towel to prevent drying out. Brush sheet of dough with oil. Spoon 3 tablespoons corned beef mixture in thin strip 1/2 inch from narrow edge of dough. Roll up dough from narrow edge to enclose filling, folding in edges. Place seam side down on baking sheet sprayed with nonstick cooking spray. Score crosswise into 4 equal portions; brush with oil. Repeat with remaining dough and corned beef mixture. Bake for 13 to 15 minutes or until brown. Cut into scored portions. Serve warm. Yield: 9 servings.

Approx Per Serving: Cal 151; Prot 9 g; Carbo 12 g; Fiber 1 g;
T Fat 8 g; 45% Calories from Fat; Chol 7 mg; Sod 217 mg.

Cajun Shrimp

1 pound extra large shrimp,
peeled
1 tablespoon lime juice
1/2 teaspoon garlic powder
1/2 teaspoon onion powder

1/4 teaspoon thyme
1/4 teaspoon salt
1/8 to 1/4 teaspoon red pepper
1/8 teaspoon black pepper

Toss shrimp with lime juice in bowl. Mix garlic powder, onion powder, thyme, salt, red pepper and black pepper in small bowl. Sprinkle over shrimp; toss to coat well. Spray large skillet with nonstick cooking spray. Heat until hot. Add shrimp. Cook for 3 minutes or until shrimp turn pink, stirring constantly. Spoon into serving dish. Chill, covered, for 1 hour or longer. Garnish with lime wedges. May double recipe or use smaller shrimp; adjust cooking time accordingly. Yield: 8 servings.

Approx Per Serving: Cal 45; Prot 9 g; Carbo <1 g; Fiber <1 g;
T Fat <1 g; 10% Calories from Fat; Chol 89 mg; Sod 168 mg.

 For a radish accordion, select long narrow radishes. Cut a thin slice from each end and cut crosswise into slices, leaving bottom intact. Chill in iced water until radish slices open.

Curried Shrimp Bundles

1   4-ounce can tiny shrimp, rinsed, drained
1/3 cup nonfat yogurt
1/4 cup finely chopped unsalted peanuts
2 tablespoons chutney, finely chopped
1/4 cup coconut
1 teaspoon curry powder
1/4 teaspoon ginger
6 sheets frozen phyllo dough, thawed
1/2 cup melted margarine

Preheat oven to 375 degrees. Combine shrimp, yogurt, peanuts, chutney and coconut in bowl; mix gently. Add curry powder and ginger; mix gently. Place 1 sheet phyllo on waxed paper-lined surface; keep remaining phyllo covered with damp cloth. Brush phyllo with margarine. Top with 2 additional sheets phyllo, brushing each with margarine. Cut stack into 4-inch squares. Place 2 teaspoons filling on each. Bring corners up to enclose filling. Repeat with remaining ingredients. Place on baking sheet lined with baking parchment or foil. Bake for 18 to 20 minutes or until golden brown. Yield: 12 servings.

Approx Per Serving: Cal 137; Prot 5 g; Carbo 9 g; Fiber 1 g;
    T Fat 10 g; 61% Calories from Fat; Chol 17 mg; Sod 163 mg.

Spinach and Cheese Triangles

8 ounces soft cream cheese with chives and onion
1   10-ounce package frozen chopped spinach, thawed, drained
Black pepper to taste
1/3 cup chopped roasted red peppers, drained
9 sheets frozen phyllo dough, thawed
6 tablespoons melted margarine

Preheat oven to 375 degrees. Combine cream cheese, spinach, black pepper and red peppers in bowl; mix well. Place 1 sheet phyllo dough on work surface, leaving remaining dough covered with damp cloth to prevent drying out. Brush sheet with margarine. Cut lengthwise into 4 equal strips. Spoon about 1 tablespoon filling 1 inch from end of each strip. Fold end over filling at 45-degree angle. Continue to fold into triangles as for flag. Repeat with remaining phyllo and filling. Place triangles on baking sheet. Brush with margarine. Bake for 12 to 15 minutes or until golden brown. Yield: 12 servings.

Approx Per Serving: Cal 170; Prot 4 g; Carbo 12 g; Fiber 1 g;
    T Fat 12 g; 63% Calories from Fat; Chol 21 mg; Sod 200 mg.

Spinach-Pita Appetizers

1 10-ounce package frozen
   chopped spinach, cooked,
   well drained
1 cup light sour cream
1 cup light mayonnaise
3 green onions, finely chopped

1 envelope vegetable soup mix
1 7-ounce can water chestnuts,
   drained, chopped
10 small pita bread rounds, cut
   into halves

Combine first 6 ingredients in bowl; mix well. Spread into pita rounds just
before serving. Yield: 20 servings.

Approx Per Serving: Cal 121; Prot 3 g; Carbo 18 g; Fiber 1 g;
       T Fat 4 g; 31% Calories from Fat; Chol 8 mg; Sod 334 mg.

Fruited Cocktail Wieners

1 16-ounce package cocktail
   wieners
1 16-ounce can sliced
   juice-pack peaches, drained
1/2 cup catsup

2 tablespoons honey
1 16-ounce can juice-pack
   pineapple chunks
1/2 teaspoon dry mustard
1/4 teaspoon allspice

Combine all ingredients in 2-quart glass dish. Microwave on High for 6 to
8 minutes or until heated through, stirring twice. Spoon into chafing dish.
Serve with toothpicks. Yield: 10 servings.

Approx Per Serving: Cal 221; Prot 6 g; Carbo 21 g; Fiber 1 g;
       T Fat 13 g; 53% Calories from Fat; Chol 23 mg; Sod 653 mg.

Melting Pot Munch

2 3-ounce cans French-fried
   onions
4 cups corn Chex cereal
2 cups Cheerios cereal
2 4-ounce cans shoestring
   potatoes

2 cups chow mein noodles
1 1/2 cups Spanish peanuts
2 1/2 ounces slivered almonds
1/2 to 3/4 envelope taco seasoning
   mix
1/2 cup melted margarine

Preheat oven to 250 degrees. Mix onions, cereals, shoestring potatoes, chow
mein noodles, peanuts, almonds and taco seasoning mix in large baking
pan. Add margarine; toss to coat well. Bake for 30 minutes, stirring every
10 minutes. Cool completely. Store in airtight container. Yield: 24 servings.

Approx Per Serving: Cal 248; Prot 5 g; Carbo 19 g; Fiber 2 g;
       T Fat 18 g; 62% Calories from Fat; Chol <1 mg; Sod 320 mg.

Light and Lively Party Mix

5 cups pretzels
4 cups bite-sized wheat or bran
   cereal squares
4 cups bite-sized shredded
   wheat cereal
3 cups oyster crackers
2 cups bite-sized round butter
   crackers
1/4 cup water

2 1/2-ounce envelopes butter
   substitute mix
1/4 cup reduced-sodium
   Worcestershire sauce
2 tablespoons canola oil
Several drops of hot pepper
   sauce
1/2 teaspoon garlic powder
1/2 teaspoon seasoned salt

Preheat oven to 300 degrees. Combine pretzels, cereals and crackers in roasting pan sprayed with nonstick cooking spray. Combine water, butter substitute mix, Worcestershire sauce, oil, pepper sauce, garlic powder and seasoned salt in saucepan. Cook until heated through, stirring to mix well. Drizzle evenly over cereal mixture; toss to mix well. Bake for 45 minutes, stirring every 15 minutes. Spread on foil to cool. Yield: 32 servings.

Approx Per Serving: Cal 136; Prot 3 g; Carbo 25 g; Fiber 2 g;
   T Fat 4 g; 26% Calories from Fat; Chol 0 mg; Sod 362 mg.

Walnut and Parmesan Bruschetta

1/2 cup Parmesan cheese
1/4 cup finely chopped walnuts
1/4 cup olive oil
1 8-ounce French bread baguette

1/2 cup olive oil
1/4 cup Parmesan cheese
1/4 cup finely chopped walnuts

Preheat oven to broil. Combine 1/2 cup Parmesan cheese, 1/4 cup walnuts and 1/4 cup olive oil in food processor container. Process until almost smooth. Cut bread diagonally into 1/2-inch slices. Brush both sides with remaining 1/2 cup olive oil. Place on baking sheet. Toast bread slices under broiler for about 30 seconds on each side. Spread with Parmesan cheese mixture. Sprinkle with remaining 1/4 cup Parmesan cheese. Press remaining 1/4 cup walnuts on top. Broil for 30 seconds or until cheese begins to melt. Yield: 8 servings.

Approx Per Serving: Cal 343; Prot 7 g; Carbo 16 g; Fiber 1 g;
   T Fat 28 g; 74% Calories from Fat; Chol 6 mg; Sod 307 mg.

Make "pincushions" of an apple, orange, pineapple or grapefruit by studding with cheese cubes and fruit on toothpicks.

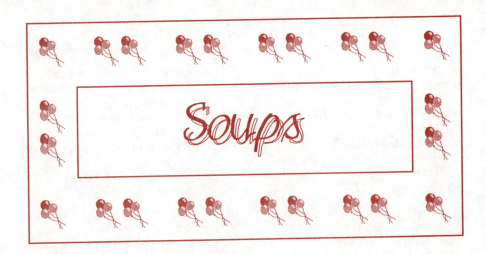

Soups

Apple Cider-Onion Soup

1¼ pounds red onions, thinly
   sliced
2 tablespoons margarine
2 tablespoons all-purpose flour
1 teaspoon minced garlic
3 cups canned beef broth
3 cups chicken broth

1 cup apple cider
1 bay leaf
1½ teaspoons thyme
Salt and pepper to taste
6   ½-inch slices French bread
2 cups shredded Swiss cheese

Sauté onions in margarine in large saucepan over medium heat until golden brown. Add flour. Cook for 2 minutes, stirring constantly. Add garlic. Cook for 1 minute. Add broths, apple cider and bay leaf. Bring to a boil; skim surface. Stir in thyme. Simmer for 40 minutes. Season with salt and pepper. Preheat broiler. Place bread on baking sheet; sprinkle with cheese. Broil just until cheese melts. Ladle soup into serving bowls, discarding bay leaf. Top with cheese toast. Yield: 6 servings.

Approx Per Serving: Cal 365; Prot 19 g; Carbo 33 g; Fiber 2 g;
    T Fat 17 g; 42% Calories from Fat; Chol 35 mg; Sod 1128 mg.

Start your summer brunch or luncheon with a cold soup. Purée 1½ cups each of cantaloupe and honeydew with 2 cups orange juice and 3 tablespoons honey. Add 2 cups white grape juice and 1½ cups each chopped cantaloupe and honeydew. Serve the soup well chilled.

Artichoke Soup

1 cup sliced green onions
1/4 cup chopped onion
2 tablespoons melted margarine
2 tablespoons all-purpose flour

1   14-ounce can chicken broth
1   14-ounce can artichoke hearts
1/4 teaspoon white pepper
2 tablespoons minced parsley

Sauté green onions and onion in margarine in saucepan until tender. Add flour. Stir in broth. Cook until thickened, stirring constantly. Drain artichokes, reserving liquid. Chop coarsely. Add artichokes, reserved liquid and white pepper to onion mixture. Cook over low heat until heated through, stirring frequently. Ladle into soup bowls. Sprinkle with parsley. Yield: 2 servings.

Approx Per Serving: Cal 253; Prot 10 g; Carbo 22 g; Fiber 2 g;
T Fat 14 g; 50% Calories from Fat; Chol 1 mg; Sod 1264 mg.

Cream of Asparagus Soup

1 pound fresh asparagus
1 cup chicken broth
1/4 cup margarine
1/4 cup all-purpose flour

2 1/2 cups chicken broth
1/2 cup evaporated skim milk
Pepper to taste

Trim asparagus; cut into 1-inch pieces. Cook in 1 cup chicken broth in medium saucepan until tender. Melt margarine in large deep saucepan. Remove from heat; blend in flour. Add 2 1/2 cups chicken broth gradually, stirring constantly. Cook over medium heat until slightly thickened, stirring constantly. Add evaporated milk, pepper, asparagus and broth. Cook until heated through, stirring frequently. Yield: 4 servings.

Approx Per Serving: Cal 230; Prot 10 g; Carbo 12 g; Fiber 2 g;
T Fat 17 g; 63% Calories from Fat; Chol 13 mg; Sod 827 mg.

Herbed White Bean Soup

1 large onion, chopped
2 cloves of garlic, minced
1 carrot, shredded
1 tablespoon canola oil
2   15-ounce cans Great Northern
   beans

1   14-ounce can chicken broth
Salt and pepper to taste
1 teaspoon dried sage
1/4 teaspoon thyme
Oregano to taste

Sauté first 3 ingredients in oil in saucepan until tender. Add undrained beans and chicken broth. Stir in remaining ingredients. Bring to a boil; reduce heat. Simmer until heated through, stirring occasionally. Yield: 4 servings.

Approx Per Serving: Cal 242; Prot 14 g; Carbo 37 g; Fiber 17 g;
T Fat 5 g; 17% Calories from Fat; Chol <1 mg; Sod 1061 mg.

Very Easy Borsch

1 envelope onion soup mix
2 16-ounce cans julienne-style
   beets
1 11-ounce can beef broth

1 16-ounce jar sweet and sour
   red cabbage
1/2 cup light sour cream

Prepare onion soup in 4-quart saucepan using package directions. Stir in undrained beets, beef broth and undrained cabbage. Simmer until heated through. Ladle into soup bowls. Top with sour cream. Yield: 8 servings.

Approx Per Serving: Cal 58; Prot 2 g; Carbo 9 g; Fiber 2 g;
    T Fat 2 g; 30% Calories from Fat; Chol 6 mg; Sod 510 mg.
    Nutritional information does not include cabbage.

Swiss Broccoli Soup

1 10-ounce package frozen
   chopped broccoli, thawed
2 stalks celery, chopped
1 onion, chopped
1 cup unsalted chicken broth
2 cups skim milk

2 tablespoons cornstarch
1/4 teaspoon salt
1/8 teaspoon pepper
1/8 teaspoon thyme
1 ounce Swiss cheese, shredded

Bring vegetables and broth to a boil in large saucepan. Simmer, covered, for 8 minutes. Add mixture of milk, cornstarch and seasonings. Cook for 4 minutes or until thickened, stirring constantly. Remove from heat. Add cheese, stirring until melted. Yield: 4 servings.

Approx Per Serving: Cal 126; Prot 10 g; Carbo 18 g; Fiber 3 g;
    T Fat 3 g; 18% Calories from Fat; Chol 8 mg; Sod 264 mg.

Cauliflower Soup

1 cup chopped celery
2 cups sliced cauliflower
1 14-ounce can chicken broth
1 cup evaporated skim milk
1 10-ounce can cream of potato
   soup

1/4 cup water
2 tablespoons cornstarch
2 cups chopped cooked ham
1/2 cup shredded sharp Cheddar
   cheese

Cook celery and cauliflower in chicken broth in saucepan for 10 minutes. Stir in evaporated milk and potato soup. Blend water and cornstarch in small bowl. Stir into soup with ham. Cook until thickened, stirring constantly. Add cheese. Simmer until cheese melts. Yield: 6 servings.

Approx Per Serving: Cal 203; Prot 20 g; Carbo 14 g; Fiber 1 g;
    T Fat 7 g; 32% Calories from Fat; Chol 40 mg; Sod 1336 mg.

Chicken-Tortellini Soup

2 cups chopped cooked chicken
3　14-ounce cans chicken broth
1 cup sliced carrot
1/4 cup chopped onion
1 cup chopped celery

1/2 cup grated Parmesan cheese
1/2 teaspoon thyme
1/4 teaspoon oregano
1　16-ounce package frozen
　cheese tortellini

Combine chicken, chicken broth, vegetables, cheese and herbs in 4-quart saucepan. Cook over medium heat for 10 minutes or until carrots and celery are tender. Add pasta. Cook for 10 minutes longer. Yield: 8 servings.

Approx Per Serving: Cal 297; Prot 24 g; Carbo 29 g; Fiber 1 g;
　T Fat 9 g; 28% Calories from Fat; Chol 63 mg; Sod 823 mg.

Mexican Chicken Soup

3 1/2 cups fresh or frozen corn
1 cup chicken broth
1/4 cup melted margarine
2 cups chopped cooked chicken
1 clove of garlic, chopped
1 teaspoon cumin
2 cups low-fat milk
1　4-ounce can chopped green
　chilies
3 dashes of Tabasco sauce

1 cup shredded jalapeño
　Monterey Jack cheese
1　12-ounce package tortilla
　chips
1 cup chopped tomatoes
1/2 cup chopped black olives
1/3 cup light sour cream
1/4 cup chopped green onions
1/2 cup salsa

Process corn and chicken broth in blender container until smooth. Combine with margarine, chicken, garlic and cumin in saucepan; mix well. Simmer for 5 minutes, stirring constantly. Stir in milk. Heat to the boiling point; reduce heat. Stir in green chilies, Tabasco sauce and cheese. Simmer until heated through. Ladle over tortilla chips in serving bowls. Top with tomatoes, olives, sour cream, green onions and salsa. Yield: 8 servings.

Approx Per Serving: Cal 517; Prot 23 g; Carbo 45 g; Fiber 5 g;
　T Fat 30 g; 50% Calories from Fat; Chol 54 mg; Sod 796 mg.

Use your slow cooker to keep soup warm for a special holiday buffet.

Cream Cheese and Corn Soup

1/3 cup finely chopped green bell
   pepper
1/4 cup finely chopped onion
1 tablespoon margarine
1 tablespoon canola oil

2 cups chicken stock
1 cup low-fat milk
1 8-ounce can cream-style corn
8 ounces light cream cheese
Salt and pepper to taste

Sauté green pepper and onion in margarine and oil in 2-quart saucepan until tender. Add next 4 ingredients. Simmer until cheese melts, stirring frequently. Season with salt and pepper. Serve hot. Yield: 4 servings.

Approx Per Serving: Cal 277; Prot 12 g; Carbo 19 g; Fiber 2 g;
     T Fat 18 g; 57% Calories from Fat; Chol 38 mg; Sod 938 mg.

Speedy White Chili

1 large white onion, chopped
1 tablespoon oil
2 15-ounce cans Great Northern
   beans
1 4-ounce can chopped green
   chilies
1 10-ounce can chicken broth

2 5-ounce cans chicken, drained
1 tablespoon garlic salt
2 1/2 teaspoons cumin
2 teaspoons oregano
2 1/2 teaspoons coriander
1/2 teaspoon cayenne pepper

Sauté onion in oil in large saucepan until tender. Add remaining ingredients; mix well. Bring to a boil; reduce heat. Simmer for 15 to 20 minutes or until heated through. Yield: 10 servings.

Approx Per Serving: Cal 128; Prot 12 g; Carbo 15 g; Fiber 7 g;
     T Fat 3 g; 17% Calories from Fat; Chol <1 mg; Sod 1181 mg.

Crab Bisque

1 onion, chopped
2 tablespoons margarine
1 10-ounce can tomato soup
1/2 cup water
Juice of 1/4 lemon
1 teaspoon sugar

1 bay leaf
8 whole cloves
1 teaspoon dill
Salt and pepper to taste
1 7-ounce can crab meat
1 cup evaporated skim milk

Sauté onion in margarine in saucepan. Stir in next 9 ingredients. Simmer for 20 minutes. Discard cloves and bay leaf. Add crab meat. Simmer just until heated through. Add enough evaporated milk to make of desired consistency and color. Simmer just until heated through. Yield: 4 servings.

Approx Per Serving: Cal 216; Prot 17 g; Carbo 21 g; Fiber 1 g;
     T Fat 8 g; 31% Calories from Fat; Chol 47 mg; Sod 799 mg.

Cheesy Ham Chowder

1 6-ounce package au gratin
    potato mix
4 cups water
2 cups chopped cabbage

1 cup chopped carrot
1 cup chopped cooked ham
1 teaspoon caraway seed
1 cup low-fat milk

Combine potatoes and seasoning packet with water, cabbage, carrot, ham and caraway seed in large saucepan; mix well. Simmer, covered, for 15 to 20 minutes or until potatoes are tender. Add milk. Simmer, uncovered, for 5 minutes longer. Yield: 6 servings.

Approx Per Serving: Cal 178; Prot 10 g; Carbo 25 g; Fiber 1 g;
     T Fat 3 g; 17% Calories from Fat; Chol 17 mg; Sod 1001 mg.

Minestrone Soup

4 slices bacon, chopped
1 large onion, chopped
1 cup chopped celery
2 10-ounce cans beef broth
4 cups water
1 cup uncooked ditalini
1 32-ounce jar spaghetti sauce
1 cup chopped carrot

1 20-ounce can chick peas
1 10-ounce package frozen
    green beans
1 cup chopped fresh parsley
1 teaspoon salt
1 teaspoon pepper
1/2 cup Parmesan cheese

Sauté bacon, onion and celery in skillet until brown; drain. Combine with beef broth and water in 5-quart saucepan. Cook for 20 minutes. Cook ditalini using package directions; drain. Add to broth with spaghetti sauce, carrot, chick peas, beans, parsley, salt and pepper. Simmer for 20 minutes, stirring occasionally. Ladle into soup bowls; sprinkle with Parmesan cheese. Yield: 10 servings.

Approx Per Serving: Cal 244; Prot 9 g; Carbo 36 g; Fiber 3 g;
     T Fat 8 g; 28% Calories from Fat; Chol 5 mg; Sod 1153 mg.

Easy Peanut Soup

1 1/2 cups cream of chicken soup
1 1/2 cups cream of celery soup

1/4 cup chunky peanut butter
1 1/2 cups water

Combine soups, peanut butter and water in 2-quart saucepan; mix well. Simmer over medium heat for 5 minutes, stirring occasionally. Yield: 4 servings.

Approx Per Serving: Cal 249; Prot 8 g; Carbo 17 g; Fiber 1 g;
     T Fat 18 g; 62% Calories from Fat; Chol 18 mg; Sod 1530 mg.

Pumpkin Soup

6 cups chicken broth
2 cups peeled cubed pumpkin
1 cup thinly sliced onion
1 clove of garlic, minced
1/2 teaspoon thyme

1/2 teaspoon salt
5 peppercorns
1/2 cup evaporated skim milk
1 teaspoon chopped parsley

Combine chicken broth, pumpkin, onion, garlic, thyme, salt and pepper-corns in saucepan. Bring to a boil. Simmer for 20 minutes. Remove and reserve 1/2 cup pumpkin mixture. Simmer remaining mixture for 20 minutes longer. Purée 2 cups of the mixture at a time in blender container. Combine in saucepan. Simmer until heated through. Stir in evaporated milk and reserved pumpkin mixture. Sprinkle with parsley. Yield: 8 servings.

Approx Per Serving: Cal 53; Prot 5 g; Carbo 5 g; Fiber 1 g;
    T Fat 1 g; 20% Calories from Fat; Chol 1 mg; Sod 734 mg.

Salmon Chowder

2 tablespoons chopped onion
2 tablespoons margarine
1 16-ounce can tomatoes,
   chopped
1 12-ounce can whole kernel
   corn

1 10-ounce can Cheddar cheese
   soup
1 cup low-fat milk
1 16-ounce can salmon,
   drained, flaked
1 tablespoon chopped parsley

Sauté onion in margarine in large saucepan until tender but not brown. Add tomatoes, undrained corn, soup and milk; mix well. Cook until heated through. Stir in salmon and parsley. Cook until heated through.
Yield: 6 servings.

Approx Per Serving: Cal 267; Prot 20 g; Carbo 18 g; Fiber 1 g;
    T Fat 14 g; 44% Calories from Fat; Chol 53 mg; Sod 1103 mg.

Ginger Shrimp Soup

4 cups chicken stock
1 teaspoon ground ginger
Salt and pepper to taste

6 green onions, chopped
16 large shrimp, peeled, cooked

Heat chicken stock with ginger, salt and pepper in saucepan until bubbly. Add green onions and shrimp; remove from heat. Let stand for 15 minutes. Heat to serving temperature. Yield: 4 servings.

Approx Per Serving: Cal 133; Prot 24 g; Carbo 2 g; Fiber <1 g;
    T Fat 2 g; 17% Calories from Fat; Chol 174 mg; Sod 976 mg.

Butternut Squash Soup

1 medium butternut squash,
 peeled, chopped
1 cup chopped celery
1 carrot, chopped

1 apple, chopped
6 cups chicken broth
1 cup evaporated skim milk

Combine squash, celery, carrot and apple with chicken broth in saucepan. Cook until vegetables are tender. Purée in blender container. Combine with enough evaporated milk to make of desired consistency in saucepan. Cook just until heated through. Yield: 8 servings.

Approx Per Serving: Cal 111; Prot 7 g; Carbo 19 g; Fiber 4 g;
 T Fat 1 g; 10% Calories from Fat; Chol 2 mg; Sod 638 mg.

Cream of Wild Rice Soup

1 large onion, finely chopped
1 carrot, finely chopped
1 stalk celery, finely chopped
3 slices turkey bacon, chopped
1/2 cup margarine

1 cup all-purpose flour
8 cups chicken broth
Salt and pepper to taste
3 cups cooked wild rice
1 cup evaporated skim milk

Sauté onion, carrot, celery and turkey bacon in margarine in 4-quart saucepan for 3 minutes. Sift in flour gradually, stirring constantly until smooth but not brown. Add broth slowly, stirring constantly. Add salt and pepper. Stir in rice. Simmer for several minutes. Add evaporated milk just before serving. Simmer until heated through. Yield: 12 servings.

Approx Per Serving: Cal 210; Prot 9 g; Carbo 23 g; Fiber 2 g;
 T Fat 9 g; 40% Calories from Fat; Chol 5 mg; Sod 692 mg.

Quick Zucchini Soup

1 pound zucchini, thickly sliced
1 medium onion, chopped

1 14-ounce can chicken broth
1 teaspoon curry powder

Cook zucchini and onion in chicken broth in medium saucepan until tender. Purée in blender container. Combine with curry powder in saucepan. Cook just until heated through. Yield: 4 servings.

Approx Per Serving: Cal 46; Prot 4 g; Carbo 7 g; Fiber 2 g;
 T Fat 1 g; 15% Calories from Fat; Chol <1 mg; Sod 319 mg.

Salads

Apple-Pineapple Salad

1   20-ounce can juice-pack
    crushed pineapple
1/2 cup sugar
3 tablespoons cornstarch
1 tablespoon vinegar

4 cups chopped apples
1 cup chopped celery
1 cup miniature marshmallows
1 cup seedless purple grapes

Combine pineapple, sugar and cornstarch in saucepan. Cook over medium heat until thickened, stirring constantly. Stir in vinegar. Let stand until cool. Stir in apples, celery, marshmallows and grapes. Yield: 8 servings.

Approx Per Serving: Cal 177; Prot 1 g; Carbo 46 g; Fiber 3 g;
    T Fat <1 g; 2% Calories from Fat; Chol 0 mg; Sod 21 mg.

Molded Ambrosia

1   6-ounce package orange gelatin
2 cups boiling water
1 pint orange sherbet
2   11-ounce cans mandarin
    oranges, drained

1 cup flaked coconut
1   16-ounce can juice-pack
    pineapple chunks, drained
1 cup miniature marshmallows
1 cup light whipped topping

Dissolve gelatin in water in bowl. Stir in sherbet and 1 can mandarin oranges. Pour into oiled 6-cup ring mold. Chill until firm. Mix remaining ingredients in bowl. Chill for 3 hours. Unmold salad onto salad plate. Spoon fruit mixture into center. Yield: 8 servings.

Approx Per Serving: Cal 308; Prot 4 g; Carbo 67 g; Fiber 2 g;
    T Fat 5 g; 14% Calories from Fat; Chol 4 mg; Sod 103 mg.

Five-Minute Fruit Salad

2 cups miniature marshmallows
1 11-ounce can mandarin
  oranges, drained
1 8-ounce can pineapple
  tidbits, drained
1 17-ounce can fruit cocktail,
  drained
1 21-ounce can lemon pie filling
8 ounces light whipped topping

Combine marshmallows, mandarin oranges, pineapple and fruit cocktail in bowl; toss lightly. Fold in pie filling and whipped topping gently. Serve immediately. Yield: 10 servings.

Approx Per Serving: Cal 164; Prot 1 g; Carbo 41 g; Fiber 2 g;
    T Fat 1 g; 5% Calories from Fat; Chol 0 mg; Sod 33 mg.

Frosty Lemon Salad

2 cups nonfat lemon yogurt
1 4-ounce package lemon
  instant pudding mix
1 cup flaked coconut
1 8-ounce can crushed
  pineapple, partially drained

Blend yogurt and pudding mix in bowl until smooth. Stir in coconut and pineapple. Spoon into 9x12-inch dish. Freeze until firm. Remove from freezer 20 minutes before serving. Yield: 20 servings.

Approx Per Serving: Cal 57; Prot 1 g; Carbo 10 g; Fiber 1 g;
    T Fat 1 g; 20% Calories from Fat; Chol <1 mg; Sod 56 mg.

Fruit-Filled Orange Ring

1 20-ounce can juice-pack
  pineapple chunks, drained
1 16-ounce can juice-pack
  sliced peaches, drained
1 11-ounce can mandarin
  oranges, drained
2 apples, peeled, chopped
3 bananas, sliced
1 4-ounce package vanilla
  instant pudding mix
1^{1}/2 cups low-fat milk
1/3 cup thawed frozen orange
  juice concentrate
3/4 cup light sour cream
8 lettuce cups

Combine pineapple, peaches, mandarin oranges, apples and bananas in large bowl. Combine pudding mix, milk and orange juice concentrate in mixer bowl. Beat at high speed for 1 to 2 minutes. Beat in sour cream. Add to fruit; mix well. Chill, covered, in refrigerator. Serve in lettuce cups. Garnish with additional orange sections. Yield: 8 servings.

Approx Per Serving: Cal 275; Prot 4 g; Carbo 60 g; Fiber 3 g;
    T Fat 4 g; 13% Calories from Fat; Chol 13 mg; Sod 135 mg.

Fruit Sampler with Yogurt Sauce

3 cups nonfat vanilla yogurt
1/4 cup honey
1 teaspoon grated orange rind
4 large navel oranges
2 apples, peeled, cored

2 pears, peeled, cored
2 kiwifruit, peeled, sliced
4 ounces seedless red grapes, in
small clusters

Combine yogurt, honey and orange rind in bowl; mix well. Chill, covered, until serving time. Cut oranges into halves horizontally. Remove orange sections carefully; reserve juice and orange shells. Cut apples and pears into wedges. Sprinkle with reserved orange juice. Spoon yogurt sauce into reserved orange shells; place on 8 individual serving plates. Arrange orange sections, apple wedges, pear wedges, kiwifruit and grapes around orange shells. Garnish with lemon leaves. Yield: 8 servings.

Approx Per Serving: Cal 174; Prot 6 g; Carbo 39 g; Fiber 4 g;
   T Fat 1 g; 3% Calories from Fat; Chol 2 mg; Sod 67 mg.

Tangy Fruit Bowl

1 20-ounce can juice-pack
   peaches
1 20-ounce can juice-pack pears
1 20-ounce can juice-pack
   pineapple chunks
Sections of 2 large oranges,
   chopped

2 large apples, chopped
4 medium bananas, sliced
2 tablespoons orange breakfast
   drink mix
1 6-ounce package vanilla
   instant pudding mix

Drain and chop peaches, pears and pineapple, reserving juices. Combine canned fruit with oranges, apples and bananas in bowl. Blend 3 cups reserved juices with orange drink mix and pudding mix in bowl. Add to fruit; mix well. Chill until serving time. Yield: 8 servings.

Approx Per Serving: Cal 295; Prot 2 g; Carbo 76 g; Fiber 6 g;
   T Fat 1 g; 2% Calories from Fat; Chol 0 mg; Sod 152 mg.

For a layered congealed salad for the Fourth of July, use cherry and blueberry gelatins separated by a cream cheese layer. May coordinate gelatin flavors to suit your holiday color scheme.

Gingered Fruit Cup

3 tablespoons lemon juice
3 tablespoons honey
1¹/₂ teaspoons oil
¹/₄ teaspoon ginger

Sections of 4 oranges
4 pears, coarsely chopped
2 red apples, coarsely chopped
1 cup golden raisins

Combine lemon juice, honey, oil and ginger in large bowl; mix well. Add oranges, pears, apples and raisins; toss to mix. Chill until serving time. Spoon into compotes. Garnish with mint leaves. Yield: 8 servings.

Approx Per Serving: Cal 207; Prot 2 g; Carbo 52 g; Fiber 7 g; T Fat 2 g; 6% Calories from Fat; Chol 0 mg; Sod 4 mg.

Healthy Heavenly Hash

1 20-ounce can juice-pack
   pineapple chunks, drained
1 11-ounce can mandarin
   oranges, drained
1 banana, sliced

1¹/₂ cups seedless grapes
1 cup miniature marshmallows
¹/₂ cup flaked coconut
¹/₄ cup chopped almonds
1 cup nonfat vanilla yogurt

Combine pineapple, mandarin oranges, banana, grapes, marshmallows, coconut and almonds in bowl; mix well. Fold in yogurt gently. Chill until serving time. Yield: 6 servings.

Approx Per Serving: Cal 246; Prot 5 g; Carbo 49 g; Fiber 3 g; T Fat 5 g; 18% Calories from Fat; Chol 1 mg; Sod 44 mg.

Anytime Peach Salad

1 21-ounce can peach pie filling
2 bananas, sliced

1 11-ounce can mandarin
   oranges, drained

Combine pie filling, bananas and mandarin oranges in bowl. Chill until serving time. Yield: 8 servings.

Approx Per Serving: Cal 120; Prot 1 g; Carbo 32 g; Fiber 2 g; T Fat <1 g; 1% Calories from Fat; Chol 0 mg; Sod 25 mg.

Delightful Pear Salad

1½ 16-ounce cans pears
1 3-ounce package lemon
gelatin

8 ounces light cream cheese,
softened
9 ounces light whipped topping

Drain pears, reserving juice. Chop pears. Bring pear juice to a boil in saucepan over medium heat. Stir in gelatin until dissolved. Remove from heat. Beat in cream cheese. Stir in pears and whipped topping. Spoon into serving dish. Chill until serving time. Yield: 12 servings.

Approx Per Serving: Cal 122; Prot 3 g; Carbo 20 g; Fiber 1 g;
T Fat 4 g; 29% Calories from Fat; Chol 11 mg; Sod 133 mg.

Heavenly Pistachio Salad

1 20-ounce can crushed
pineapple
1 4-ounce package pistachio
instant pudding mix

2 cups small curd light cottage
cheese
12 ounces light whipped topping

Mix undrained pineapple and pudding mix in bowl. Stir in cottage cheese and whipped topping. Chill until serving time. Yield: 12 servings.

Approx Per Serving: Cal 122; Prot 5 g; Carbo 22 g; Fiber 1 g;
T Fat 2 g; 13% Calories from Fat; Chol 3 mg; Sod 217 mg.

Holiday Ribbon Salad

1 3-ounce package strawberry
gelatin
¾ cup boiling water
1 14-ounce jar cranberry-orange
relish
2 tablespoons lemon juice

1 tablespoon grated orange rind
1 envelope unflavored gelatin
1 cup cold water
8 ounces light cream cheese
2 tablespoons lemon juice
2 cups light whipped topping

Dissolve strawberry gelatin in boiling water in bowl. Add relish, 2 table-spoons lemon juice and orange rind; mix well. Pour into lightly oiled 6-cup mold. Chill until partially set. Sprinkle unflavored gelatin over cold water in small saucepan. Let stand for 1 minute to soften. Cook over low heat until gelatin is dissolved, stirring constantly; remove from heat. Combine soft-ened cream cheese and 2 tablespoons lemon juice in mixer bowl; beat until fluffy. Fold in whipped topping and unflavored gelatin mixture. Spread evenly over cranberry layer. Chill until firm. Unmold onto lettuce-lined serving plate. Yield: 10 servings.

Approx Per Serving: Cal 183; Prot 4 g; Carbo 31 g; Fiber 1 g;
T Fat 5 g; 26% Calories from Fat; Chol 13 mg; Sod 170 mg.

Cottage Raspberries

2 cups light cottage cheese
1 3-ounce package raspberry
   gelatin

8 ounces light whipped topping
1 cup raspberries

Combine cottage cheese and dry gelatin in bowl; mix well. Fold in whipped topping and raspberries. Chill until serving time. Yield: 10 servings.

Approx Per Serving: Cal 92; Prot 7 g; Carbo 12 g; Fiber 1 g;
      T Fat 2 g; 17% Calories from Fat; Chol 4 mg; Sod 211 mg.

Raspberry Aspic

2 16-ounce cans stewed
   tomatoes
2 3-ounce packages raspberry
   gelatin

3/4 cup boiling water
Hot pepper sauce to taste
8 lettuce leaves

Process undrained tomatoes in blender until coarsely chopped. Dissolve gelatin in boiling water in bowl. Add tomatoes and hot pepper sauce; mix well. Pour into oiled 6-cup mold. Chill until firm. Unmold onto lettuce-lined serving plate. Yield: 8 servings.

Approx Per Serving: Cal 117; Prot 3 g; Carbo 28 g; Fiber <1 g;
      T Fat <1 g; 0% Calories from Fat; Chol 0 mg; Sod 434 mg.

Cranberry Waldorf Salad

1 12-ounce package cranberries
2 cups miniature marshmallows
3/4 cup sugar
1 cup seedless grapes

3 cups chopped unpeeled tart
   apples
1/2 cup chopped walnuts
2 cups light whipped topping

Process cranberries in food processor until finely chopped. Combine with marshmallows and sugar in bowl; mix well. Chill overnight. Add grapes, apples and walnuts to cranberry mixture; mix well. Fold in whipped topping gently. Spoon into serving dish. Chill until serving time.
Yield: 10 servings.

Approx Per Serving: Cal 210; Prot 1 g; Carbo 42 g; Fiber 3 g;
      T Fat 6 g; 23% Calories from Fat; Chol 0 mg; Sod 12 mg.

Smoked Chicken Salad

3 tablespoons balsamic vinegar
1 teaspoon fresh basil
1 teaspoon fresh marjoram
1/2 cup extra-virgin olive oil
Salt to taste
Freshly ground pepper to taste
1 head each Boston and Bibb
  lettuce, torn

1 bunch watercress
1 pound smoked chicken
Sections of 1 large pink
  grapefruit
1 avocado, peeled, sliced
2 tablespoons sunflower seed or
  toasted pine nuts

Process first 6 ingredients in food processor until smooth. Combine with lettuce and watercress in plastic bag; shake to coat. Arrange greens, chicken, grapefruit and avocado on serving plate. Drizzle with remaining dressing; sprinkle with sunflower seed. Yield: 6 servings.

Approx Per Serving: Cal 407; Prot 24 g; Carbo 11 g; Fiber 5 g;
  T Fat 30 g; 66% Calories from Fat; Chol 68 mg; Sod 74 mg.

Chicken and Rice Salad

2 cups chopped cooked chicken
2 cups cooked rice
1 cup chopped celery
1/4 cup chopped green bell pepper
1/4 cup chopped green onions

1/4 cup light mayonnaise
1 envelope ranch salad dressing
  mix
1/2 teaspoon seasoned salt
6 lettuce cups

Mix chicken, rice, celery, bell pepper, green onions, mayonnaise, salad dressing mix and salt in bowl. Serve in lettuce cups. Yield: 6 servings.

Approx Per Serving: Cal 205; Prot 15 g; Carbo 22 g; Fiber 1 g;
  T Fat 6 g; 25% Calories from Fat; Chol 44 mg; Sod 542 mg.

Ham Salad

8 ounces medium pasta shells,
  cooked, drained
1 1/2 cups chopped cooked ham
1/2 cup sliced celery
1/2 cup sliced radishes
1 cup sliced cucumber

1/2 cup light mayonnaise
1/2 cup plain nonfat yogurt
2 teaspoons Dijon mustard
1 teaspoon garlic salt
4 lettuce cups

Combine first 5 ingredients in salad bowl. Mix mayonnaise, yogurt, mustard and garlic salt in small bowl. Add to salad; toss to mix well. Chill until serving time. Serve in lettuce cups. Yield: 4 servings.

Approx Per Serving: Cal 399; Prot 23 g; Carbo 53 g; Fiber 4 g;
  T Fat 10 g; 23% Calories from Fat; Chol 37 mg; Sod 1467 mg.

Golden Tuna Salad

1/4 cup sliced almonds
2 6-ounce cans water-pack
   white tuna
1/4 cup thinly sliced green onions
1 19-ounce can juice-pack
   pineapple chunks, drained
1/2 cup sliced celery

1/2 cup light mayonnaise
1 teaspoon reduced-sodium soy
   sauce
Ginger to taste
1/4 teaspoon salt
4 cups salad greens

Preheat oven to 350 degrees. Sprinkle almonds in single layer in baking pan. Toast for 5 minutes or until golden brown. Drain tuna, reserving liquid. Combine tuna, almonds, green onions, pineapple, celery and 2 or 3 drops of reserved tuna liquid; mix well. Blend mayonnaise, soy sauce, ginger and salt in small bowl. Add to salad; mix gently. Chill until serving time. Serve on salad greens. Garnish with tomatoes. Yield: 4 servings.

Approx Per Serving: Cal 312; Prot 28 g; Carbo 29 g; Fiber 3 g;
    T Fat 10 g; 28% Calories from Fat; Chol 56 mg; Sod 693 mg.

Summer Tuna Salad

1 large crown summer squash
1/4 cup light French salad
   dressing
1 head lettuce, torn
1 cup flaked tuna, chilled
1 cup chopped celery

1 cup cooked green beans, peas
   or carrots, chilled
1 green bell pepper, minced
2 tomatoes, sliced
2 hard-cooked eggs, sliced

Boil or steam squash in saucepan until tender. Scoop out seed and center pulp. Drizzle with French salad dressing. Chill in refrigerator. Place squash on bed of lettuce on serving plate. Combine tuna, celery, beans and green pepper in bowl. Add enough French salad dressing to make of desired consistency; mix well. Spoon into squash. Alternate tomato slices and egg slices in overlapping layer around edge. Garnish with parsley. Yield: 4 servings.

Approx Per Serving: Cal 183; Prot 19 g; Carbo 13 g; Fiber 4 g;
    T Fat 6 g; 30% Calories from Fat; Chol 29 mg; Sod 535 mg.

Make a summer patio salad bar by placing the ingredients for the salad in clean flowerpots of different sizes.

Bombay Turkey Salad

8 ounces cooked turkey breast, chopped
1 11-ounce can mandarin oranges, drained
1 banana, sliced

2 tablespoons (about) lemon juice
1/4 cup light mayonnaise
2 tablespoons orange juice
1/2 teaspoon curry powder
6 cups salad greens

Combine turkey and mandarin oranges in bowl. Sprinkle banana with lemon juice. Add banana and mixture of mayonnaise, orange juice and curry powder to salad; mix gently. Chill until serving time. Serve on crisp salad greens. Yield: 6 servings.

Approx Per Serving: Cal 144; Prot 13 g; Carbo 17 g; Fiber 1 g;
    T Fat 4 g; 21% Calories from Fat; Chol 29 mg; Sod 83 mg.

Fiesta Turkey Salad

1 cup light mayonnaise
1 tablespoon lemon juice
1 4-ounce can chopped green chilies
1/4 cup sliced black olives
1 tablespoon chili powder
1/2 teaspoon salt

2 cups chopped cooked turkey
3 1/2 cups cooked rice, chilled
8 lettuce cups
2 tomatoes, chopped
2 avocados, chopped
1/4 cup chopped black olives
1 8-ounce package corn chips

Mix mayonnaise, lemon juice, chilies, 1/4 cup sliced black olives, chili powder and salt in bowl. Add turkey and rice; mix well. Chill until serving time. Serve in lettuce cups. Top with tomatoes, avocados, 1/4 cup chopped black olives and corn chips. Yield: 8 servings.

Approx Per Serving: Cal 496; Prot 16 g; Carbo 49 g; Fiber 8 g;
    T Fat 27 g; 49% Calories from Fat; Chol 35 mg; Sod 741 mg.

Fresh Broccoli Salad

1 bunch broccoli, chopped
1 15-ounce can kidney beans, drained
1 cup shredded sharp Cheddar cheese

1 small red onion, finely chopped
1 cup light Italian salad dressing

Combine broccoli, kidney beans, cheese and onion in large bowl; mix well. Add dressing; mix well. Chill, covered, in refrigerator until serving time. Yield: 8 servings.

Approx Per Serving: Cal 133; Prot 8 g; Carbo 13 g; Fiber 6 g;
    T Fat 6 g; 41% Calories from Fat; Chol 17 mg; Sod 521 mg.

Hail Caesar Salad

1 cup light mayonnaise
2 cloves of garlic, crushed
2 tablespoons lemon juice
2 tablespoons grated Parmesan
   cheese

1 teaspoon Dijon mustard
Salt and pepper to taste
2 bunches romaine lettuce
1/2 cup Melba toast crumbs
1 cup cauliflowerets

Combine mayonnaise, garlic, lemon juice, cheese, mustard, salt and pepper in small bowl; mix well. Pour over lettuce, tossing to coat. Top with toast crumbs and cauliflowerets. Yield: 8 servings.

Approx Per Serving: Cal 126; Prot 4 g; Carbo 14 g; Fiber 2 g;
   T Fat 7 g; 48% Calories from Fat; Chol 9 mg; Sod 274 mg.

Carrot Ambrosia

1 pound carrots, shredded
1   20-ounce can juice-pack
   crushed pineapple
3/4 cup golden raisins

3/4 cup flaked coconut
3/4 cup miniature marshmallows
1 cup light sour cream
2 tablespoons honey

Combine carrots, pineapple, raisins, coconut and marshmallows in salad bowl; mix well. Add sour cream and honey; mix gently. Chill until serving time. Yield: 10 servings.

Approx Per Serving: Cal 175; Prot 2 g; Carbo 34 g; Fiber 4 g;
   T Fat 5 g; 24% Calories from Fat; Chol 10 mg; Sod 33 mg.

Citrus Green Salad

1/2 cup oil
1/3 cup fresh lemon juice
1 tablespoon honey
1 teaspoon dry mustard
Salt and pepper to taste
1/2 teaspoon paprika
1 teaspoon reduced-sodium
   Worcestershire sauce
1/4 cup chopped chives

4 cups torn salad greens
1/4 cup chopped celery
1 tart apple, thinly sliced
1/2 cucumber, thinly sliced
2 oranges, seeded, sliced
   crosswise
Sections of 1 grapefruit
1/2 cup croutons
1/4 cup crumbled bleu cheese

Combine oil, lemon juice, honey, mustard, seasonings, Worcestershire sauce and chives in covered jar; shake well. Chill in refrigerator. Arrange salad greens, celery, apple, cucumber and fruit on salad plates. Drizzle with dressing. Top with croutons and bleu cheese. Yield: 4 servings.

Approx Per Serving: Cal 411; Prot 5 g; Carbo 35 g; Fiber 5 g;
   T Fat 30 g; 63% Calories from Fat; Chol 5 mg; Sod 175 mg.

Molded Gazpacho Salad

1½ tablespoons unflavored
  gelatin
¼ cup cold water
1½ cups vegetable juice cocktail
1 medium cucumber, peeled,
  finely chopped
1 green bell pepper, finely
  chopped
4 medium tomatoes, peeled,
  chopped
¼ cup chopped green onions

¾ cup finely chopped celery
½ teaspoon Tabasco sauce
1½ tablespoons lemon juice
1½ tablespoons vinegar
1 teaspoon dillweed
1 teaspoon salt
Pepper to taste
2 tablespoons olive oil
½ cup light mayonnaise
½ cup light sour cream

Soften gelatin in cold water in cup. Bring vegetable juice cocktail to a boil in 3-quart saucepan. Stir in gelatin until dissolved. Cool slightly. Add cucumber, green pepper, tomatoes, green onions, celery, Tabasco sauce, lemon juice, vinegar, dillweed, salt and pepper; mix well. Coat 6-cup mold with olive oil. Spoon in gelatin mixture. Chill until firm. Unmold onto serving plate. Mix mayonnaise and sour cream in bowl. Serve with salad. Yield: 8 servings.

Approx Per Serving: Cal 133; Prot 2 g; Carbo 8 g; Fiber 1 g;
    T Fat 8 g; 54% Calories from Fat; Chol 10 mg; Sod 525 mg.

Holiday Salad Bowl

2 tablespoons wine vinegar
½ teaspoon salt
Pepper to taste
½ teaspoon tarragon
½ teaspoon chervil
2 teaspoons chopped parsley
1 shallot, finely chopped
2 teaspoons chopped chives
1½ teaspoons Dijon mustard

3 tablespoons light whipping
  cream
3 tablespoons light sour cream
3 tablespoons oil
1 head Boston lettuce
1 head romaine lettuce
2 cloves of garlic
1 slice bread, toasted

Combine vinegar, salt, pepper, tarragon, chervil, parsley, shallot, chives, mustard, whipping cream, sour cream and oil in blender container. Process until smooth. Chill for several hours. Tear salad greens into bite-sized pieces. Rub salad bowl with 1 clove of garlic. Rub toast with remaining garlic; cut into croutons. Place salad greens and croutons in prepared salad bowl. Add creamy tarragon dressing; toss lightly. Yield: 6 servings.

Approx Per Serving: Cal 128; Prot 2 g; Carbo 7 g; Fiber 1 g;
    T Fat 11 g; 72% Calories from Fat; Chol 11 mg; Sod 247 mg.

Party Salad

1 clove of garlic
1 head lettuce
1/2 bunch romaine lettuce
1 bunch watercress
1/4 cup slivered toasted almonds

Flowerets of 1 small head
  cauliflower
1 avocado, chopped
1 large tomato, peeled, chopped
1 cup celery seed dressing

Rub salad bowl with garlic. Tear greens into bowl. Add almonds, cauliflowerets, avocado and tomato; mix well. Add celery seed dressing just before serving. Yield: 8 servings.

Approx Per Serving: Cal 224; Prot 3 g; Carbo 14 g; Fiber 5 g;
    T Fat 20 g; 73% Calories from Fat; Chol 0 mg; Sod 245 mg.

Country Potato and Bean Salad

4 red potatoes, cooked, cut into
  quarters
8 ounces green beans, sliced,
  cooked

Basil, chives and seasoned salt
  to taste
1/2 cup light Ranch salad dressing

Combine potatoes, beans, seasonings and enough salad dressing to moisten in large bowl; mix well. Chill until serving time. Yield: 8 servings.

Approx Per Serving: Cal 159; Prot 3 g; Carbo 30 g; Fiber 3 g;
    T Fat 4 g; 22% Calories from Fat; Chol 5 mg; Sod 130 mg.

Romaine Salad

1 head romaine lettuce, torn
1 2-ounce can sliced black
  olives, drained
2 oranges, peeled, thinly sliced
1/4 cup orange juice

2 teaspoons red wine vinegar
1/4 cup olive oil
1/4 teaspoon paprika
1/2 teaspoon salt

Combine lettuce, olives and oranges in salad bowl. Mix remaining ingredients in small bowl. Add to salad; toss lightly. Yield: 4 servings.

Approx Per Serving: Cal 189; Prot 2 g; Carbo 11 g; Fiber 3 g;
    T Fat 17 g; 75% Calories from Fat; Chol 0 mg; Sod 378 mg.

Mandarin Spinach Salad

3/4 cup light mayonnaise
2 tablespoons honey
1 tablespoon lemon juice
1 tablespoon caraway seed
10 ounces fresh spinach, torn
1 head iceberg lettuce, torn
2 tablespoons chopped onion

2 tablespoons chopped green
  bell pepper
2 tablespoons chopped pimento
1 11-ounce can mandarin
  oranges, drained
1 cucumber, sliced

Combine mayonnaise, honey, lemon juice and caraway seed in bowl; mix
well. Combine remaining ingredients in large salad bowl. Add salad dressing; toss to mix well. Yield: 12 servings.

Approx Per Serving: Cal 76; Prot 1 g; Carbo 12 g; Fiber 2 g;
    T Fat 3 g; 36% Calories from Fat; Chol 4 mg; Sod 98 mg.

Tortellini Salad

1 9-ounce package spinach and
  cheese tortellini
2 cups frozen mixed broccoli,
  carrot and cauliflower

1/2 cup light ranch salad dressing
1/2 teaspoon Italian seasoning
1/4 cup grated Parmesan cheese

Cook pasta using package directions. Drain over vegetables in colander.
Mix vegetables, pasta and salad dressing in bowl. Add Italian seasoning
and cheese; toss to mix well. Chill until serving time. Yield: 10 servings.

Approx Per Serving: Cal 129; Prot 5 g; Carbo 15 g; Fiber 1 g;
    T Fat 6 g; 38% Calories from Fat; Chol 18 mg; Sod 237 mg.
    Nutritional information does not include Italian seasoning.

Vegetables in Mustard Vinaigrette

Flowerets of 1 head cauliflower
Flowerets of 1 head broccoli
1 1/3 pounds asparagus
1 pound green beans
5 1/3 ounces snow peas
1 pound carrots, cut into sticks
1/3 cup Dijon mustard

1/3 cup tarragon vinegar
1 cup olive oil
1 shallot, minced
Salt and freshly ground pepper
  to taste
Chopped herbs such as parsley,
  tarragon, chervil or dill to taste

Blanch and chill vegetables. Whisk mustard and vinegar in bowl. Add oil
gradually, whisking constantly. Add shallot, seasonings and herbs. Serve
over vegetables. Yield: 8 servings.

Approx Per Serving: Cal 354; Prot 8 g; Carbo 22 g; Fiber 8 g;
    T Fat 29 g; 69% Calories from Fat; Chol 0 mg; Sod 311 mg.

Main Events

Step right this way for the greatest, easiest main dishes ever collected between two covers! Beef that will dazzle you! Ground beef in fabulous variations! Poultry that will take your breath away! Light and delicious pork dishes to tantalize any appetite! Seafood delights from the briny deep to astound you! Casseroles to captivate you and your guests! Try one—try all. Our Main Events are what you've been waiting for so that the center ring of your celebration will bring delight and applause.

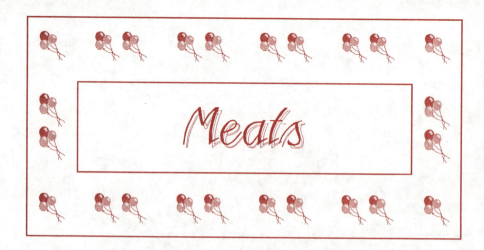

Beef with Cider and Mushrooms

1¹/₂ pounds round steak, cubed
1 10-ounce can reduced-sodium golden mushroom soup
1 4-ounce can sliced mushrooms, drained

1 envelope onion soup mix
¹/₂ cup apple cider
1 16-ounce package noodles, cooked

Combine steak, mushroom soup, mushrooms, onion soup mix and apple cider in slow cooker. Cook on Low for 6 to 8 hours. Serve over noodles. Yield: 4 servings.

Approx Per Serving: Cal 736; Prot 49 g; Carbo 89 g; Fiber 1 g;
     T Fat 18 g; 23% Calories from Fat; Chol 295 mg; Sod 360 mg.

Beef Fajitas

1 pound flank steak, ¹/₂ inch thick
³/₄ cup fresh lime juice
1 teaspoon garlic salt
¹/₂ teaspoon pepper
16 small flour tortillas, warmed

1 large tomato, chopped
3 bunches green onions, chopped
3 cups shredded Cheddar cheese
1 cup each guacamole, picante sauce and light sour cream

Place beef in plastic bag. Sprinkle both sides with lime juice, garlic salt and pepper; tie bag securely. Marinate in refrigerator; drain. Grill steak over medium-hot coals for 2 to 3 minutes on each side. Cut cross grain into thin slices. Serve in tortillas with remaining ingredients. Yield: 8 servings.

Approx Per Serving: Cal 578; Prot 29 g; Carbo 51 g; Fiber 4 g;
     T Fat 31 g; 46% Calories from Fat; Chol 89 mg; Sod 1195 mg.

Mushroom-Topped Tenderloins

4 3/4-inch tenderloin steaks
2 tablespoons margarine
Salt and pepper to taste
1 1/2 cups chopped mushrooms

1/4 cup sliced green onions
1/2 teaspoon minced garlic
1/4 teaspoon marjoram
1/8 teaspoon pepper

Brown steaks in margarine in large skillet over high heat for 6 to 8 minutes or until done to taste, turning once. Remove to warm serving plate; sprinkle with salt and pepper to taste. Add mushrooms, green onions, garlic, marjoram and 1/8 teaspoon pepper to drippings in skillet. Cook over medium heat for 4 minutes or until mushrooms are tender. Spoon over steaks. Yield: 4 servings.

Approx Per Serving: Cal 251; Prot 28 g; Carbo 2 g; Fiber 1 g;
T Fat 14 g; 51% Calories from Fat; Chol 81 mg; Sod 113 mg.

Peppered Beef Tenderloin Roast

5 cloves of garlic, finely chopped
2 tablespoons finely chopped
    fresh rosemary
1 tablespoon green peppercorns
    in brine, drained, finely
    chopped
Salt to taste

1 teaspoon freshly ground
    pepper
1 4-pound beef tenderloin,
    trimmed
2 tablespoons olive oil
1 1/4 cups beef stock

Combine garlic, rosemary, peppercorns, salt and pepper in small bowl. Rub over roast. Wrap tightly in plastic wrap. Marinate for 4 to 48 hours. Preheat oven to 425 degrees. Let roast stand until room temperature. Brown roast in olive oil in large Dutch oven for 4 minutes on each side. Place rack in Dutch oven; place roast on rack. Insert meat thermometer in thickest part of beef. Roast, uncovered, for 10 to 12 minutes per pound or until meat thermometer registers 135 degrees for rare or 155 degrees for medium. Allow for internal temperature to increase by about 5 degrees after removal from oven. Let stand in warm place for 15 minutes. Stir beef stock into pan drippings in Dutch oven. Simmer until reduced to 3/4 cup. Strain into serving bowl. Serve with roast. Yield: 12 servings.

Approx Per Serving: Cal 223; Prot 29 g; Carbo 1 g; Fiber <1 g;
T Fat 11 g; 46% Calories from Fat; Chol 85 mg; Sod 128 mg.
Nutritional information does not include green peppercorns
in brine.

Orange and Spice Pot Roast

3 slices bacon
1 4-pound eye-of-round roast
2 tablespoons lemon juice
Salt to taste
1 8-ounce can tomatoes
1 cup orange juice
2/3 cup chopped onion
1 teaspoon sugar

1 tablespoon parsley flakes
1 teaspoon cinnamon
4 whole cloves
1 clove of garlic, minced
1 bay leaf
2 tablespoons all-purpose flour
1/4 cup cold water

Preheat oven to 325 degrees. Brown bacon in Dutch oven. Remove bacon; crumble. Sprinkle roast with lemon juice and salt. Brown on all sides in bacon drippings; drain. Mix bacon, tomatoes, orange juice, onion, sugar and seasonings in bowl. Pour over roast. Roast, covered, for 3 hours or until tender. Remove roast to heated serving platter. Discard cloves and bay leaf; skim fat. Stir in mixture of flour and water. Cook until thickened, stirring constantly. Serve with roast. Yield: 8 servings.

Approx Per Serving: Cal 346; Prot 44 g; Carbo 8 g; Fiber 1 g;
T Fat 14 g; 38% Calories from Fat; Chol 130 mg; Sod 154 mg.

Steak Bonne Femme

1/2 large red onion, thinly sliced
  into rings
10 medium mushrooms, sliced
1/2 clove of garlic, minced
1 1/2 teaspoons margarine
1 1/2 teaspoons oil

2 6-ounce top sirloin steaks, 3/4
  inch thick
2 tablespoons beef broth
Salt and freshly ground pepper
  to taste

Warm ovenproof platter in 200-degree oven. Sauté onion rings, mushrooms and garlic in margarine and oil in large skillet until tender. Increase heat. Sauté until onion rings are brown and juices have evaporated. Remove with slotted spoon. Add steaks and additional margarine and oil if necessary. Cook for 3 to 4 minutes on each side for rare. Remove to warm platter. Add broth to skillet, stirring to deglaze. Cook until liquid is reduced to desired consistency; reduce heat. Add onion mixture. Cook until heated through. Season with salt and pepper. Spoon over steaks. Yield: 2 servings.

Approx Per Serving: Cal 317; Prot 35 g; Carbo 7 g; Fiber 2 g;
T Fat 17 g; 47% Calories from Fat; Chol 96 mg; Sod 139 mg.

Decorate meat platters with bundles of herbs used in preparing the dish such as oregano, basil, thyme, rosemary, sage or parsley.

Easy Beef Stroganoff

12 ounces sirloin steak
2 tablespoons oil
4   4-ounce cans sliced
    mushrooms
1 medium onion, chopped
2 cups beef broth

2 tablespoons reduced-sodium
    Worcestershire sauce
1/2 cup tomato sauce
1/2 teaspoon paprika
11/2 cups uncooked instant rice
1/2 cup light sour cream

Cut steak into thin strips. Brown in oil in skillet. Add mushrooms and onion. Sauté for 3 minutes or until onion is tender. Add next 4 ingredients. Bring to a boil. Cook for 3 minutes. Stir in rice. Let stand, covered, for 5 minutes. Stir in sour cream. Yield: 4 servings.

Approx Per Serving: Cal 410; Prot 24 g; Carbo 43 g; Fiber 4 g;
    T Fat 16 g; 35% Calories from Fat; Chol 60 mg; Sod 1127 mg.

Steak Stroganoff

2 tablespoons all-purpose flour
1/2 teaspoon garlic powder
1/4 teaspoon paprika
1/2 teaspoon pepper
11/4 pounds boneless beef round
    steak
1 envelope onion soup mix

1   10-ounce can reduced-sodium
    cream of mushroom soup
1/2 cup water
1   9-ounce jar sliced
    mushrooms, drained
1/2 cup light sour cream

Mix flour, garlic powder, paprika and pepper in slow cooker. Trim beef; cut into 1-inch strips. Add to flour mixture; toss to coat well. Add soup mix, mushroom soup and water; mix well. Cook on Low for 6 to 7 hours or on High for 3 to 31/2 hours. Stir in mushrooms and sour cream. Cook on High for 10 to 15 minutes or just until heated through. Serve with beef-flavored rice and a spinach salad. Yield: 6 servings.

Approx Per Serving: Cal 208; Prot 20 g; Carbo 8 g; Fiber 1 g;
    T Fat 10 g; 44% Calories from Fat; Chol 61 mg; Sod 330 mg.

Teriyaki Flank Steak

13/4 cups reduced-sodium soy sauce
2 tablespoons crushed garlic

1 teaspoon ginger
2 pounds flank steak

Combine soy sauce, garlic and ginger in shallow dish. Add steak, coating well. Marinate for 1 hour. Place steak on rack in broiler pan or on grill. Broil or grill for 10 minutes on each side. Yield: 4 servings.

Approx Per Serving: Cal 233; Prot 29 g; Carbo 9 g; Fiber <1 g;
    T Fat 9 g; 34% Calories from Fat; Chol 85 mg; Sod 1867 mg.

Corned Beef Burgers

1 12-ounce can corned beef, flaked
3 tablespoons finely chopped onion
2 tablespoons prepared mustard

2 tablespoons light mayonnaise-type salad dressing
2 teaspoons prepared horseradish
8 sandwich buns
8 slices Colby cheese

Preheat broiler. Mix first 5 ingredients in bowl. Spread over bottom halves of buns. Arrange on baking sheet. Broil just until heated through. Top with cheese. Broil until cheese melts. Replace tops of buns. Yield: 8 servings.

Approx Per Serving: Cal 361; Prot 22 g; Carbo 25 g; Fiber 1 g; T Fat 19 g; 47% Calories from Fat; Chol 64 mg; Sod 938 mg.

Vienna Burgers

1 pound lean ground chuck
1/3 cup chili sauce
1 1/2 teaspoons prepared mustard
2 teaspoons prepared horseradish
1 teaspoon minced onion
1 1/2 teaspoons reduced-sodium Worcestershire sauce

1 teaspoon salt
Pepper to taste
1 loaf Vienna bread
2 tablespoons margarine, softened
4 ounces shredded sharp cheese
Oregano to taste

Preheat broiler. Combine first 8 ingredients in bowl; mix well. Cut bread into halves lengthwise. Spread each half with margarine. Spread ground chuck mixture over margarine layer. Place in broiler pan. Broil for 6 minutes or until ground chuck is brown. Sprinkle with cheese and oregano. Broil until cheese melts. Cut into serving pieces. Yield: 6 servings.

Approx Per Serving: Cal 494; Prot 27 g; Carbo 43 g; Fiber 3 g; T Fat 24 g; 44% Calories from Fat; Chol 69 mg; Sod 1224 mg.

Cheeseburger and Fries Casserole

2 pounds lean ground beef
1 10-ounce can reduced-sodium golden mushroom soup

1 10-ounce can reduced-sodium Cheddar cheese soup
1 20-ounce package frozen French fries

Preheat oven to 350 degrees. Brown ground beef in skillet, stirring until crumbly; drain. Spoon into 9x13-inch baking pan. Pour mixture of soups over ground beef. Arrange French fries over top. Bake for 45 to 55 minutes or until potatoes are golden brown. Garnish with pickles and catsup. Yield: 6 servings.

Approx Per Serving: Cal 695; Prot 34 g; Carbo 44 g; Fiber 2 g; T Fat 43 g; 55% Calories from Fat; Chol 110 mg; Sod 651 mg.

Grilled Hamburgers In-Style

1½ pounds lean ground beef
1¼ teaspoons Italian seasoning
¾ teaspoon garlic powder
½ teaspoon onion powder

¼ teaspoon salt
2 ounces mozzarella cheese, cut
  into 4 pieces

Combine ground beef, Italian seasoning, garlic powder, onion powder and salt in bowl; mix well. Shape into eight ¼-inch patties. Place cheese in center of 4 patties; top with remaining patties, sealing edge. Grill over medium-hot coals until done to taste, turning once. Yield: 4 servings.

French-Style: Prepare as above, using lean ground beef with ½ teaspoon onion powder, 1 teaspoon thyme, ½ teaspoon garlic powder, ¼ teaspoon salt, ¼ teaspoon pepper and 2 ounces Brie or Camembert cheese.

Mexican-Style: Prepare as above, using lean ground beef with 1 tablespoon chili powder, ½ teaspoon ground cumin, ½ teaspoon onion powder, ¼ teaspoon garlic powder, ¼ teaspoon salt and 2 ounces Monterey Jack Cheese.

Greek-Style: Prepare as above, using lean ground beef with 1½ teaspoons onion powder, 1 teaspoon oregano, ½ teaspoon garlic powder, ¼ teaspoon pepper and 2 ounces feta cheese mixed with 1 tablespoon lemon juice.

Approx Per Serving: Cal 388; Prot 34 g; Carbo 1 g; Fiber <1 g;
    T Fat 27 g; 63% Calories from Fat; Chol 122 mg; Sod 284 mg.
    Nutritional information does not include Italian seasonings
    and variations.

Baked Enchiladas

1 10-ounce can mild enchilada
   sauce
1 12-ounce can evaporated skim
   milk
1 10-ounce can reduced-
   sodium cream of mushroom
   soup

1 4-ounce can chopped green
   chilies
2 cups cooked lean ground beef
2 cups shredded Cheddar cheese
10 small flour tortillas
4 cups chopped lettuce
2 cups chopped tomatoes

Preheat oven to 350 degrees. Combine enchilada sauce, evaporated milk, soup and green chilies in bowl; mix well. Spoon 1 to 2 tablespoons sauce mixture, ground beef and cheese onto each tortilla. Roll up to enclose filling. Place into 9x13-inch baking pan. Top with remaining sauce and cheese. Bake, covered with foil, for 15 to 20 minutes. Top with lettuce and tomatoes. Yield: 5 servings.

Approx Per Serving: Cal 597; Prot 28 g; Carbo 66 g; Fiber 4 g;
    T Fat 24 g; 36% Calories from Fat; Chol 57 mg; Sod 1266 mg.

Easy Lasagna

1 pound lean ground beef,
  crumbled
1 48-ounce jar spaghetti sauce
1/2 cup water
1 1/4 cups ricotta cheese
1 egg, slightly beaten
1/2 teaspoon salt
1/2 teaspoon pepper
9 uncooked lasagna noodles
8 ounces mozzarella cheese,
  thinly sliced
1/2 cup grated Parmesan cheese

Microwave ground beef in glass bowl on High for 2 to 3 minutes or until no longer pink; drain. Add spaghetti sauce and water; mix well. Microwave on High for 4 to 5 minutes or until bubbly. Mix ricotta cheese, egg, salt and pepper in bowl. Spoon 1/2 cup ricotta cheese mixture into 9x13-inch glass dish. Layer noodles, remaining ricotta cheese mixture, mozzarella cheese and meat sauce 1/3 at a time in prepared dish. Microwave, covered with plastic wrap, on High for 10 minutes. Microwave on Medium for 35 minutes or until noodles are tender. Sprinkle with Parmesan cheese. Let stand, covered, for 15 minutes before serving. Yield: 8 servings.

Approx Per Serving: Cal 600; Prot 31 g; Carbo 53 g; Fiber 2 g;
    T Fat 30 g; 45% Calories from Fat; Chol 109 mg; Sod 1253 mg.

Grilled Meat Loaf

2 pounds lean ground beef
1 egg, beaten
1 onion, chopped
1/4 cup catsup
2 tablespoons light brown sugar
1/2 cup cracker crumbs
1 teaspoon prepared mustard
3 tablespoons light brown sugar
1/4 cup catsup
1 teaspoon dry mustard
1/4 teaspoon nutmeg

Combine ground beef, egg, onion, 1/4 cup catsup, 2 tablespoons brown sugar, cracker crumbs and prepared mustard in large bowl; mix well. Shape into loaf; place in lightly greased 10-inch baking pan. Grill over hot coals for 15 minutes. Place double thickness of foil on grill. Remove loaf to foil. Grill for 10 minutes longer, basting with mixture of 3 tablespoons brown sugar, 1/4 cup catsup, dry mustard and nutmeg. Yield: 6 servings.

Approx Per Serving: Cal 426; Prot 30 g; Carbo 24 g; Fiber 1 g;
    T Fat 23 g; 49% Calories from Fat; Chol 137 mg; Sod 442 mg.

Italian Rolled Meat Loaf

1½ pounds lean ground beef
1 egg, slightly beaten
1 teaspoon salt
¼ teaspoon pepper

3 slices boiled ham
2 slices mozzarella cheese
½ cup chopped green olives

Combine ground beef, egg, salt and pepper in large bowl; mix well. Pat into 8x11-inch rectangle ½ inch thick on waxed paper. Arrange ham slices crosswise on beef mixture; top with cheese slices. Sprinkle with chopped olives. Roll up as for jelly roll, sealing edge. Place seam side down in 5x9-inch glass loaf pan. Insert microwave meat thermometer into center of loaf. Microwave on High for 5 minutes or to 105 degrees on thermometer. Microwave on Medium for 16 minutes or to 135 degrees on thermometer. Microwave on Medium-Low for 4 minutes or to 155 degrees on thermometer. Yield: 6 servings.

Approx Per Serving: Cal 316; Prot 28 g; Carbo 1 g; Fiber 1 g;
T Fat 23 g; 64% Calories from Fat; Chol 125 mg; Sod 762 mg.

Festive Roll-Up

1 pound lean ground beef
½ cup finely chopped celery
¼ cup chopped onion
1 tablespoon reduced-sodium
   Worcestershire sauce
¼ cup catsup
1 egg, beaten

¼ cup oats
Salt to taste
2 cups baking mix
1 tablespoon chopped parsley
1 teaspoon dry mustard
½ cup low-fat milk

Preheat oven to 375 degrees. Brown ground beef in skillet, stirring until crumbly; drain. Add celery, onion, Worcestershire sauce, catsup, egg, oats and salt; mix well. Combine baking mix, parsley, mustard and milk in large bowl, stirring to moisten. Knead gently 8 to 10 times on lightly floured surface. Roll to 10x12-inch rectangle. Spread ground beef mixture to within ½ inch of edges. Roll up as for jelly roll. Seal edge; turn under ends. Place on greased baking sheet. Bake for 20 to 25 minutes or until golden brown. Serve with prepared gravy or chili sauce and salad or vegetables. Yield: 8 servings.

Approx Per Serving: Cal 292; Prot 15 g; Carbo 27 g; Fiber 1 g;
T Fat 14 g; 43% Calories from Fat; Chol 65 mg; Sod 549 mg.

Pizza Casserole

1 pound lean ground beef
1 small onion, chopped
1/3 cup chopped green bell
   pepper
1 clove of garlic, minced
1 4-ounce can mushrooms,
   drained
1/2 cup chopped pepperoni
1/2 cup sliced black olives

1 6-ounce can tomato paste
2 cups uncooked noodles
2 cups water
1 teaspoon salt
1/8 teaspoon each pepper, basil
   and oregano
1/4 cup grated Parmesan cheese
1 cup shredded mozzarella
   cheese

Combine ground beef, onion, green pepper and garlic in 2-quart glass baking dish. Microwave on High for 5 to 6 minutes or until ground beef is crumbly; drain. Add mushrooms, pepperoni, olives, tomato paste, noodles, water and seasonings; mix well. Microwave for 20 minutes or until noodles are tender, stirring 2 to 3 times. Sprinkle with cheeses. Microwave until cheeses are melted. Yield: 6 servings.

Approx Per Serving: Cal 361; Prot 24 g; Carbo 16 g; Fiber 3 g;
      T Fat 23 g; 57% Calories from Fat; Chol 86 mg; Sod 911 mg.

Potato Crust Pizza

1 5-ounce package scalloped
   potatoes
1 14-ounce can tomato purée
1 1/2 cups water
1 teaspoon Italian seasoning

1 pound lean ground chuck
1 4-ounce package sliced
   pepperoni
8 ounces mozzarella cheese,
   shredded

Preheat oven to 400 degrees. Arrange potatoes in 10x10-inch baking dish; sprinkle with sauce mix. Combine tomato purée, water and Italian seasoning in saucepan; mix well. Bring to a boil. Pour over potatoes. Brown ground chuck in skillet, stirring until crumbly; drain. Spoon over tomato sauce. Layer with pepperoni slices; sprinkle with cheese. Bake for 30 to 35 minutes. Yield: 4 servings.

Approx Per Serving: Cal 592; Prot 40 g; Carbo 16 g; Fiber 2 g;
      T Fat 40 g; 62% Calories from Fat; Chol 128 mg; Sod 990 mg.
      Nutritional information does not include Italian seasoning.

Inside-Out Ravioli Casserole

1 pound lean ground beef
1/2 cup chopped onion
1 clove of garlic, minced
1 tablespoon oil
1 10-ounce package frozen
   chopped spinach
1 16-ounce jar spaghetti sauce
1 8-ounce can tomato sauce

1 6-ounce can tomato paste
Salt and pepper to taste
7 ounces shell macaroni, cooked
4 ounces American cheese,
   shredded
1/2 cup bread crumbs
2 eggs, beaten
1/4 cup oil

Preheat oven to 350 degrees. Brown ground beef with onion and garlic in 1 tablespoon oil in skillet, stirring until ground beef is crumbly; drain. Cook spinach using package directions. Drain, reserving liquid. Add enough water to liquid to equal 1 cup. Add to ground beef mixture with spaghetti sauce, tomato sauce, tomato paste, salt and pepper; mix well. Simmer, covered, for 10 minutes. Combine macaroni, cheese, bread crumbs, eggs, remaining 1/4 cup oil and spinach; mix well. Spread mixture in 9x13-inch baking dish. Top with meat sauce. Bake for 30 minutes. Let stand for 10 minutes before serving. Yield: 6 servings.

Approx Per Serving: Cal 641; Prot 30 g; Carbo 55 g; Fiber 6 g;
   T Fat 35 g; 48% Calories from Fat; Chol 139 mg; Sod 1062 mg.

Baked Spaghetti Pie

7 ounces spaghetti, cooked
2 tablespoons margarine
1/3 cup grated Parmesan cheese
2 eggs, well beaten
1 cup low-fat cottage cheese
1 pound lean ground beef

1/2 cup chopped onion
1/4 cup chopped green bell
   pepper
1 15-ounce jar spaghetti sauce
1/2 cup shredded mozzarella
   cheese

Preheat oven to 350 degrees. Mix spaghetti, margarine, Parmesan cheese and eggs in bowl. Press firmly into 10-inch pie plate. Spread with cottage cheese. Brown ground beef, onion and green pepper in skillet, stirring frequently; drain. Stir in spaghetti sauce; spread over cottage cheese layer. Top with mozzarella cheese. Bake for 20 minutes. May prepare ahead and freeze. Bake for 35 to 40 minutes if frozen. Yield: 8 servings.

Approx Per Serving: Cal 375; Prot 23 g; Carbo 30 g; Fiber 2 g;
   T Fat 18 g; 44% Calories from Fat; Chol 101 mg; Sod 552 mg.

Fifteen-Minute Ground Beef Stroganoff

1 onion, minced
1 clove of garlic, minced
1/4 cup margarine
1 1/2 pounds lean ground beef
1 pound mushrooms, sliced
2 tablespoons all-purpose flour
1 1/2 teaspoons salt

1/2 teaspoon paprika
1/4 teaspoon pepper
1   10-ounce can reduced-sodium
   cream of chicken soup
1 cup light sour cream
8 ounces egg noodles, cooked

Sauté onion and garlic in margarine in 12-inch skillet for 3 minutes. Add ground beef, mushrooms, flour, salt, paprika and pepper. Cook until ground beef is brown, stirring frequently. Add soup. Bring to a boil; reduce heat to low. Simmer for 5 minutes, stirring often. Stir in sour cream just before serving. Serve over cooked noodles. Garnish with chopped parsley. Yield: 6 servings.

Approx Per Serving: Cal 565; Prot 31 g; Carbo 40 g; Fiber 2 g;
    T Fat 32 g; 50% Calories from Fat; Chol 161 mg; Sod 920 mg.

Grilled Lamb Chops

2 lamb chops, trimmed
1 tablespoon olive oil

1/4 teaspoon pepper
1/2 teaspoon salt

Sprinkle lamb chops with olive oil and pepper. Grill over hot coals for 3 1/2 to 4 minutes on each side or until done to taste. Sprinkle with salt. Yield: 2 servings.

Approx Per Serving: Cal 215; Prot 21 g; Carbo 0 g; Fiber 0 g;
    T Fat 13 g; 59% Calories from Fat; Chol 66 mg; Sod 593 mg.

Lamb Chops Parmesan

8 lamb chops
1/2 cup grated Parmesan cheese
1 teaspoon lemon juice

2 tablespoons margarine, softened
1/2 teaspoon oregano
Salt and pepper to taste

Preheat broiler. Arrange chops on rack in broiler pan. Broil 2 inches from heat source for 3 minutes on each side. Combine cheese, lemon juice, margarine, oregano, salt and pepper in small bowl; mix well. Spread mixture on 1 side of chops. Broil for 4 minutes longer or until cheese is light brown. Yield: 4 servings.

Approx Per Serving: Cal 407; Prot 46 g; Carbo 1 g; Fiber <1 g;
    T Fat 22 g; 51% Calories from Fat; Chol 141 mg; Sod 375 mg.

Asparagus Ham Rolls

4 1½-ounce slices Swiss cheese
8 1-ounce thin slices boiled
   ham
1 15-ounce can long asparagus
   spears, drained

1 10-ounce can reduced-sodium
   Cheddar cheese soup
2 tablespoons water
¼ teaspoon celery salt
¼ cup sliced almonds

Layer ½ slice cheese on each ham slice. Top with 2 or 3 asparagus spears. Roll as for jelly roll. Place seam side down in 8x12-inch glass dish. Combine soup, water and celery salt in bowl; mix well. Spoon over ham rolls. Microwave, covered with plastic wrap, on High for 5 to 7 minutes or until heated through. Sprinkle with almonds. Yield: 8 servings.

Approx Per Serving: Cal 198; Prot 17 g; Carbo 7 g; Fiber 1 g;
    T Fat 12 g; 54% Calories from Fat; Chol 43 mg; Sod 745 mg.

Holiday Ham in-a-Hurry

2 8-ounce slices cooked ham
1 8-ounce can sliced pineapple

4 maraschino cherries
2 tablespoons light brown sugar

Preheat oven to 350 degrees. Line 9x13-inch baking pan with foil. Place ham slices in prepared pan. Drain pineapple, reserving 2 tablespoons juice. Arrange pineapple on ham slices with maraschino cherry in center of each ring. Sprinkle with brown sugar. Drizzle with reserved pineapple juice. Fold foil over to seal. Bake for 25 minutes. Yield: 4 servings.

Approx Per Serving: Cal 254; Prot 29 g; Carbo 20 g; Fiber 1 g;
    T Fat 6 g; 23% Calories from Fat; Chol 62 mg; Sod 1509 mg.

Tortellini with Ham and Broccoli

¾ cup margarine, softened
1 teaspoon basil
½ teaspoon garlic powder
¼ teaspoon pepper
2 tablespoons light mayonnaise
4 ounces light cream cheese, cubed

½ cup evaporated skim milk
1 cup grated Parmesan cheese
8 ounces cheese tortellini, cooked
1½ cups chopped cooked ham
1 cup chopped cooked broccoli
1 tomato, chopped

Preheat oven to 350 degrees. Combine margarine, seasonings, mayonnaise, cream cheese and evaporated milk in large bowl; mix well. Fold in Parmesan cheese, tortellini, ham and broccoli. Spoon into 9x9-inch casserole. Bake for 25 minutes. Top with chopped tomato. Bake for 5 minutes longer. Yield: 8 servings.

Approx Per Serving: Cal 389; Prot 19 g; Carbo 19 g; Fiber 1 g;
    T Fat 27 g; 62% Calories from Fat; Chol 46 mg; Sod 964 mg.

Apricot-Glazed Pork Roast

1   4-pound boneless, rolled pork
    loin roast
1 teaspoon salt
1/4 teaspoon pepper
1 3/4 cups herb-seasoned stuffing
    mix
1/2 cup hot water
1   12-ounce bottle of barbecue
    sauce
1   8-ounce jar apricot preserves

Preheat oven to 325 degrees. Separate roast into 2 pieces. Season with salt
and pepper. Spoon mixture of stuffing mix and hot water down center of
bottom piece. Replace top. Tie at 3-inch intervals with string. Place roast on
rack in roasting pan. Insert meat thermometer. Roast for 1 1/2 hours. Brush
with mixture of barbecue sauce and preserves. Roast for 1 hour longer or to
160 degrees on meat thermometer. Place on serving plate; remove string.
Serve with remaining sauce. Yield: 10 servings.

Approx Per Serving: Cal 388; Prot 38 g; Carbo 28 g; Fiber <1 g;
    T Fat 13 g; 31% Calories from Fat; Chol 111 mg; Sod 743 mg.

Sweet and Spicy Pork Chops

4 thickly sliced pork chops
2 tablespoons oil
4 slices pineapple
2 maraschino cherries, cut into
    halves
1/2 cup apricot preserves
1/4 cup reduced-sodium soy sauce
1/4 cup white grape juice

Preheat oven to 350 degrees. Brown pork chops on both sides in oil in
skillet. Arrange in 9x9-inch shallow baking dish. Place pineapple slice and
cherry half on each pork chop. Combine preserves, soy sauce and white
grape juice in small bowl; mix well. Pour over pork chops. Bake, covered,
for 45 minutes or until pork chops are cooked through. Arrange on serving
platter. Serve with sauce. Garnish with orange slices and watercress.
Yield: 4 servings.

Approx Per Serving: Cal 451; Prot 32 g; Carbo 42 g; Fiber 1 g;
    T Fat 17 g; 34% Calories from Fat; Chol 98 mg; Sod 473 mg.

Pork Tenderloin with Artichokes

2 9-ounce packages frozen
   artichoke hearts
1 1¼-pound pork tenderloin,
   cut into 8 medallions
2 tablespoons margarine

1½ tablespoons chopped scallion
1 tablespoon capers
¼ cup chicken broth
1 teaspoon Dijon mustard

Cook artichoke hearts using package directions. Drain and rinse with cold water; set aside. Press pork medallions to 1-inch thickness. Chill until just before serving time. Brown medallions in margarine in skillet for 4 to 6 minutes on each side or until cooked through. Remove from skillet; keep warm. Add scallion and capers to pan juices. Cook for 2 minutes, stirring frequently. Add chicken broth, mustard and artichoke hearts. Cook just until heated through. Arrange medallions on serving plates. Spoon artichoke mixture over top. Yield: 4 servings.

Approx Per Serving: Cal 316; Prot 33 g; Carbo 12 g; Fiber 10 g;
   T Fat 16 g; 44% Calories from Fat; Chol 87 mg; Sod 285 mg.
   Nutritional information does not include capers.

Sausage and Apple Rings

24 ounces pork sausage
4 large cooking apples, cored
⅔ cup sugar

1 teaspoon cinnamon
¼ cup margarine
¼ cup chopped fresh parsley

Shape sausage into patties ¼ inch thick and 3½ inches in diameter. Cook in 12-inch skillet over medium heat for 10 to 15 minutes or until brown on both sides. Remove to warm plate; drain and wipe skillet. Cut ends off of apples; cut each apple into 3 slices. Coat with mixture of sugar and cinnamon. Brown a few at a time in margarine in skillet, turning frequently and sprinkling with remaining cinnamon-sugar. Place on sausage patties. Top with parsley. Yield: 12 servings.

Approx Per Serving: Cal 218; Prot 5 g; Carbo 22 g; Fiber 2 g;
   T Fat 12 g; 50% Calories from Fat; Chol 22 mg; Sod 390 mg.

Easy Sausage Cassoulet

12 ounces cooked Polish sausage
1 small onion, chopped
1 clove of garlic, minced
1 tablespoon oil
1/4 cup white grape juice
1/2 teaspoon thyme

1/8 teaspoon pepper
1   16-ounce can pork and beans
    in tomato sauce
1   15-ounce can Great Northern
    beans, drained
1 tablespoon chopped parsley

Slice sausage lengthwise; cut into 3-inch pieces. Cook with onion and garlic in oil in skillet for 3 to 4 minutes or until onion is tender. Add grape juice. Cook over low heat for 2 to 3 minutes. Stir in thyme, pepper, undrained pork and beans and Great Northern beans. Simmer for 10 minutes. Serve hot, sprinkled with parsley. Yield: 4 servings.

Approx Per Serving: Cal 378; Prot 18 g; Carbo 43 g; Fiber 15 g;
     T Fat 17 g; 38% Calories from Fat; Chol 36 mg; Sod 1219 mg.

Cheesy Sausage and Egg Puff

6 eggs, slightly beaten
1 pound sausage, browned,
    drained
1 cup buttermilk baking mix

1 cup shredded Cheddar cheese
2 cups low-fat milk
1 teaspoon dry mustard

Preheat oven to 350 degrees. Combine all ingredients in bowl; mix well. Pour into greased 2-quart casserole. Bake for 50 minutes or until knife inserted in center comes out clean. Serve with fresh fruit. Yield: 10 servings.

Approx Per Serving: Cal 250; Prot 13 g; Carbo 12 g; Fiber 0 g;
     T Fat 17 g; 60% Calories from Fat; Chol 161 mg; Sod 570 mg.

Breakfast Quiche

10 slices whole wheat bread, cut
    into quarters
3/4 cup shredded sharp cheese
2 cups cooked sausage
3 tablespoons chopped onion

1 medium zucchini, grated
6 eggs
2 cups low-fat milk
1 teaspoon salt
1/4 cup melted margarine

Line bottom and edges of greased 9x12-inch casserole with bread. Layer cheese, sausage, onion and zucchini over bread. Mix eggs, milk, salt and melted margarine in bowl. Pour mixture over top. Chill overnight. Preheat oven to 400 degrees. Bake for 50 minutes. Yield: 6 servings.

Approx Per Serving: Cal 492; Prot 25 g; Carbo 28 g; Fiber 4 g;
     T Fat 32 g; 58% Calories from Fat; Chol 262 mg; Sod 1374 mg.

Fast Veal Parmigiana

6 frozen veal patties
2 tablespoons margarine
1   15-ounce can tomatoes,
     drained, chopped
1 tablespoon dried minced onion
1 teaspoon sugar

1 teaspoon each oregano and basil
1/2 teaspoon salt
1/4 teaspoon pepper
6 slices mozzarella cheese
3 tablespoons grated Parmesan
     cheese

Brown veal patties in margarine in skillet; drain on paper towels. Add tomatoes, onion, sugar and seasonings to skillet; mix well. Cook for 5 to 10 minutes, stirring frequently. Place mozzarella cheese slice on each veal patty. Place in skillet. Sprinkle with Parmesan cheese. Cook, covered, over medium heat for 10 minutes or until cheese is melted. Yield: 6 servings.

Approx Per Serving: Cal 253; Prot 19 g; Carbo 9 g; Fiber 1 g;
     T Fat 16 g; 55% Calories from Fat; Chol 57 mg; Sod 642 mg.

Tyrolean Veal Scallopini

4 very thin slices boiled ham
4 thin veal scallops
4 teaspoons prepared mustard
1 teaspoon thyme
2 thin slices Swiss cheese

1 egg
1/4 teaspoon oregano
1/2 teaspoon salt
1/2 cup dry bread crumbs
2 tablespoons oil

Layer 1 slice of ham on each veal scallop. Spread ham with mustard; sprinkle with thyme. Cut cheese slices into halves. Place 1/2 cheese slice on top. Roll veal to enclose filling; secure with wooden pick. Beat egg with oregano and salt in shallow dish. Dip veal rolls in egg mixture; coat with bread crumbs. Fry in hot oil in skillet for 10 minutes or until golden brown on all sides. Yield: 4 servings.

Approx Per Serving: Cal 284; Prot 28 g; Carbo 10 g; Fiber 1 g;
     T Fat 14 g; 46% Calories from Fat; Chol 146 mg; Sod 696 mg.

Trim a serving platter with cucumber flowers. Cut a cucumber into thin crosswise slices. Roll up slices tightly into a flower shape, overlapping to form petals. Secure with a wooden pick and soak in salted iced water.

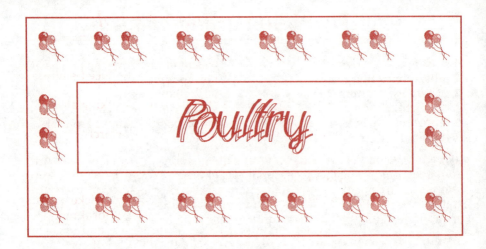

Poultry

Quicky Chicky Tortillas

3 tablespoons lime juice
1/4 teaspoon ground chilies
1 clove of garlic, minced
1 teaspoon instant chicken
   bouillon
12 ounces chicken breast filets
1 small onion, thinly sliced into
   rings
1 green bell pepper, cut into
   1/4-inch strips

1 tablespoon oil
1 cup canned corn, drained
1   15-ounce jar chunky salsa,
   drained
1   15-ounce can refried beans
6 large flour tortillas
3/4 cup shredded Cheddar cheese

Combine lime juice, chilies, garlic and chicken bouillon in shallow dish;
mix well. Rinse chicken; pat dry. Marinate in lime juice mixture in
refrigerator. Sauté onion rings and green pepper strips in oil in skillet until
tender-crisp; drain. Combine corn and salsa in small saucepan. Simmer
until heated through. Drain chicken, reserving marinade. Grill over hot
coals for 15 minutes, turning and basting frequently with reserved
marinade. Cut into strips. Combine with sautéed vegetables. Spread refried
beans in center of each tortilla. Top with chicken mixture and cheese. Roll
up to enclose filling. Top with salsa-corn mixture. Yield: 6 servings.

Approx Per Serving: Cal 452; Prot 27 g; Carbo 58 g; Fiber 9 g;
   T Fat 14 g; 27% Calories from Fat; Chol 51 mg; Sod 1332 mg.

Gingered Chicken and Broccoli

1 pound chicken breast filets,
  cut into strips
1/2 teaspoon salt
Pepper to taste
1/4 cup oil
1 pound broccoli, cut into 2-inch
  flowerets
1/2 cup sliced celery
1 16-ounce can chicken broth
1/2 teaspoon ginger
1 1/2 tablespoons reduced-sodium
  soy sauce
1 1/2 tablespoons cooking sherry
1 teaspoon sugar
1 tablespoon cornstarch
2 tablespoons water
1 cup rice, cooked

Rinse chicken; pat dry. Season with salt and pepper. Stir-fry chicken in hot oil in wok for 3 minutes. Add broccoli and celery. Stir-fry for 3 minutes. Combine chicken broth, ginger, soy sauce, cooking sherry and sugar in bowl; mix well. Stir into chicken mixture. Blend in mixture of cornstarch and water. Bring to a boil. Cook for 1 minute, stirring constantly. Serve over hot rice. May adjust seasonings to suit personal taste and may add other vegetables such as onions and mushrooms. Yield: 4 servings.

Approx Per Serving: Cal 500; Prot 36 g; Carbo 48 g; Fiber 5 g;
  T Fat 18 g; 33% Calories from Fat; Chol 73 mg; Sod 884 mg.

Chicken Breasts Cacciatore

1 16-ounce can whole tomatoes,
  chopped
1/2 medium green bell pepper,
  cut into strips
1 medium onion, cut into rings
1/4 cup chicken broth
1 1/2 teaspoons Italian seasoning
4 chicken breasts
7 ounces vermicelli, cooked
2 tablespoons grated Romano
  cheese

Combine tomatoes, green pepper, onion, chicken broth and Italian seasoning in glass bowl. Microwave, covered, on High for 5 to 7 minutes, stirring once. Rinse chicken and pat dry. Arrange in 2-quart glass dish with meatier portions toward outer edge. Pour sauce over top. Microwave for 14 to 18 minutes or until chicken is cooked through, spooning sauce over chicken once. Toss vermicelli with Romano cheese. Serve chicken and sauce over vermicelli. Yield: 4 servings.

Approx Per Serving: Cal 375; Prot 36 g; Carbo 46 g; Fiber 4 g;
  T Fat 5 g; 12% Calories from Fat; Chol 75 mg; Sod 333 mg.

Chicken Breasts Diane

4 boneless chicken breasts
1/2 teaspoon salt
1/4 teaspoon pepper
2 tablespoons melted margarine
2 tablespoons oil
Juice of 1/2 lemon

3 tablespoons chopped green
  onions
3 tablespoons chopped parsley
2 teaspoons Dijon mustard
1/4 cup chicken broth

Rinse chicken; pat dry. Place between sheets of plastic wrap; pound lightly. Sprinkle with salt and pepper. Combine margarine and oil in glass dish. Place chicken in dish, coating each piece with mixture. Microwave on High for 3 minutes. Let stand for 1 minute. Turn chicken over. Microwave for 3 minutes longer or until tender; do not overcook. Combine next 4 ingredients in glass bowl. Microwave on High for 1 minute. Stir in broth and any chicken pan juices. Pour over chicken. Serve immediately. Yield: 4 servings.

Approx Per Serving: Cal 262; Prot 27 g; Carbo 1 g; Fiber <1 g;
    T Fat 16 g; 56% Calories from Fat; Chol 72 mg; Sod 513 mg.

Walnut Chicken

2 pounds boneless chicken
  breasts, skinned
1   6-ounce package stuffing mix

6 ounces hot pepper cheese,
  shredded
1 1/2 cups chopped walnuts

Preheat oven to 350 degrees. Rinse chicken; pat dry. Prepare stuffing mix using package directions. Layer chicken and cheese in greased 3-quart baking dish. Spoon stuffing mix over top. Sprinkle with walnuts. Bake, covered, for 35 minutes. Bake, uncovered, for 10 minutes longer. Yield: 4 servings.

Approx Per Serving: Cal 886; Prot 75 g; Carbo 39 g; Fiber 3 g;
    T Fat 48 g; 49% Calories from Fat; Chol 183 mg; Sod 925 mg.

Honey-Glazed Chicken

4 chicken breasts
3 tablespoons melted margarine
1 1/2 cups chicken broth
1/4 cup finely chopped onion

2/3 cup honey
1/2 cup lemon juice
1/3 cup reduced-sodium soy sauce

Rinse chicken; pat dry. Brown in margarine in skillet. Combine chicken broth, onion, honey, lemon juice and soy sauce in 4-cup glass bowl; mix well. Microwave on High until mixture boils. Pour over chicken. Simmer, covered, until chicken is tender, basting 3 to 5 times. Yield: 4 servings.

Approx Per Serving: Cal 422; Prot 29 g; Carbo 52 g; Fiber <1 g;
    T Fat 12 g; 25% Calories from Fat; Chol 73 mg; Sod 977 mg.

Lemony Pecan Chicken

1¹/₂ pounds boneless chicken
   breasts, skinned
1 cup chopped fresh parsley
¹/₂ cup grated Parmesan cheese
¹/₃ cup oil

¹/₂ cup pecan pieces
3 tablespoons lemon juice
3 tablespoons fresh basil leaves
2 cloves of garlic, chopped

Preheat oven to 350 degrees. Rinse chicken; pat dry. Arrange chicken in 8x12-inch baking pan. Combine ²/₃ cup parsley, ¹/₃ cup Parmesan cheese, oil, ¹/₃ cup pecans, lemon juice, basil and garlic in blender container. Process until blended. Spread over chicken. Chop remaining parsley. Combine with remaining Parmesan cheese and remaining pecans in bowl. Sprinkle over casserole. Bake for 30 minutes. May microwave on High for 4 to 6 minutes or until cooked through. Yield: 6 servings.

Approx Per Serving: Cal 354; Prot 31 g; Carbo 4 g; Fiber 1 g;
     T Fat 24 g; 61% Calories from Fat; Chol 77 mg; Sod 194 mg.

Mustard-Baked Chicken

6 chicken breast filets
Salt and freshly ground pepper
   to taste
2 tablespoons light brown sugar

¹/₂ cup prepared mustard
1 clove of garlic, minced
¹/₂ teaspoon dry mustard
1¹/₂ cups bread crumbs

Preheat oven to 400 degrees. Rinse chicken and pat dry. Place on rack in roasting pan. Bake for 10 to 15 minutes or until brown. Season with salt and pepper. Combine brown sugar, prepared mustard, garlic and dry mustard in bowl; mix well. Spread over chicken. Coat with crumbs. Place on rack in roasting pan. Bake for 20 minutes; turn chicken over. Bake for 30 minutes longer or until chicken is tender and golden brown. Yield: 6 servings.

Approx Per Serving: Cal 273; Prot 31 g; Carbo 24 g; Fiber 1 g;
     T Fat 5 g; 18% Calories from Fat; Chol 73 mg; Sod 510 mg.

Make a frosted fruit garnish of grapes, cranberries or cherries. Dip the fruit into egg white beaten until frothy, then into granulated sugar; shake off excess sugar and allow to dry.

Chicken and Broccoli Stir-Fry

4 chicken breast filets
3 tablespoons peanut oil
1 large onion, sliced
1 large green bell pepper, thinly
  sliced
1 teaspoon garlic powder
1 10-ounce package frozen
  broccoli, thawed

1/4 cup water
3 tablespoons reduced-sodium
  soy sauce
1 teaspoon cornstarch
1/2 teaspoon ginger

Rinse chicken; pat dry. Cut into 1-inch strips. Stir-fry in hot oil in wok for 2 minutes. Add onion, green pepper and garlic powder. Stir-fry for 2 minutes. Add broccoli. Stir-fry for 1 minute. Cook, covered, over low heat for 5 minutes, stirring occasionally. Stir in mixture of remaining ingredients. Bring to a boil. Cook for 1 minute longer or until thickened, stirring constantly. Serve over rice. Yield: 4 servings.

Approx Per Serving: Cal 274; Prot 29 g; Carbo 9 g; Fiber 3 g;
    T Fat 13 g; 44% Calories from Fat; Chol 72 mg; Sod 374 mg.

Easy Chicken Stir-Fry

2 chicken breast filets
2 tablespoons oil
1 10-ounce package frozen
  Oriental vegetables, thawed
2 tablespoons water
3 tablespoons dry cooking sherry

1 teaspoon grated gingerroot
3 tablespoons chicken broth
2 tablespoons reduced-sodium
  soy sauce
1 1/2 teaspoons cornstarch

Rinse chicken; pat dry. Cut into 3-inch strips. Stir-fry in hot oil in wok for 1 minute. Add vegetables. Stir-fry for 1 1/2 minutes. Add water. Simmer, covered, for 2 minutes, stirring once. Mix cooking sherry, gingerroot, chicken broth, soy sauce and cornstarch in small bowl. Add to wok. Cook until sauce thickens, stirring constantly. Yield: 4 servings.

Approx Per Serving: Cal 186; Prot 15 g; Carbo 9 g; Fiber <1 g;
    T Fat 8 g; 41% Calories from Fat; Chol 36 mg; Sod 285 mg.

 For green onion frills, cut off the root end and most of the stem portion of green onions. Make narrow lengthwise cuts at both ends with sharp knife to produce a fringe. Chill in iced water until ends curl.

Peachy Chicken Breasts

6 whole chicken breasts, boned,
  skinned
1/8 teaspoon pepper
11/2 teaspoons salt
3 fresh peaches, peeled, chopped
1/2 cup chopped onion
1/2 cup coarsely chopped cashews

1/8 teaspoon ginger
1/2 cup melted margarine
1 fresh peach, peeled, sliced
1 cup light sour cream
1/2 cup packed light brown sugar
2 teaspoons Dijon mustard
1/4 teaspoon salt

Rinse chicken; pat dry. Flatten to 1/4-inch thickness between sheets of waxed paper. Sprinkle with pepper and 1 teaspoon salt; set aside. Combine remaining 1/2 teaspoon salt with chopped peaches, onion, cashews and ginger in bowl; mix well. Spoon 1/4 cup filling into center of each chicken breast. Roll up, securing with wooden picks. Pour melted margarine into 9x13-inch baking dish. Arrange chicken in dish. Bake for 25 minutes; turn. Bake for 20 minutes longer. Combine sliced peach, sour cream, brown sugar, mustard and 1/4 teaspoon salt in saucepan; mix well. Cook over low heat until heated through, stirring frequently. Serve with chicken. Yield: 6 servings.

Approx Per Serving: Cal 644; Prot 56 g; Carbo 34 g; Fiber 2 g;
    T Fat 31 g; 44% Calories from Fat; Chol 160 mg; Sod 999 mg.

Walnut-Stuffed Chicken Breasts

12 chicken breast filets
11/2 cups shredded Cheddar
  cheese
1 cup chopped walnuts
1 cup fresh bread crumbs
1/4 cup minced onion
1 teaspoon salt

1/4 teaspoon pepper
3/4 cup all-purpose flour
6 tablespoons margarine
3 cups chicken stock
2 cups white grape juice
1/4 cup chopped parsley

Wash chicken filets and pat dry. Pound 1/4 inch thick between waxed paper. Combine cheese, walnuts, bread crumbs, onion, salt and pepper in bowl; mix well. Spoon mixture onto chicken filets, spreading to within 1/2 inch of edges. Roll each as for jelly roll from narrow end; secure with toothpicks. Coat with flour. Let stand for 10 minutes. Brown lightly in margarine in large skillet. Add chicken stock and grape juice. Simmer, covered, over low heat for 20 minutes. Remove chicken to warm platter; discard toothpicks. Cook liquid in skillet until reduced to desired consistency, stirring frequently. Stir in chopped parsley. Pour over chicken. Garnish with sprigs of parsley. Yield: 12 servings.

Approx Per Serving: Cal 388; Prot 34 g; Carbo 17 g; Fiber 1 g;
    T Fat 20 g; 47% Calories from Fat; Chol 87 mg; Sod 612 mg.

Chicken Lasagna

4 cups chopped cooked chicken
1/2 cup chopped celery
1/2 cup chopped green bell
  pepper
1/2 cup chopped onion
2 cups sliced mushrooms
2 10-ounce cans reduced-sodium
  cream of mushroom soup

1/2 cup plus 2 tablespoons
  low-fat milk
1 1/2 cups shredded Cheddar
  cheese
1 1/2 cups shredded mozzarella
  cheese
14 uncooked lasagna noodles

Preheat oven to 350 degrees. Spray square 4-quart baking dish with non-stick cooking spray. Combine chicken, celery, green pepper, onion, mushrooms, soup and milk in large bowl; mix well. Combine cheeses; toss lightly. Alternate layers of chicken mixture, noodles and cheese in baking dish until all ingredients are used. Bake for 30 to 45 minutes or until noodles are tender. Yield: 9 servings.

Approx Per Serving: Cal 372; Prot 32 g; Carbo 12 g; Fiber 1 g;
  T Fat 20 g; 51% Calories from Fat; Chol 98 mg; Sod 420 mg.

Custard Chicken Loaf

1 loaf stale bread, cubed
3 tablespoons evaporated skim
  milk
3 tablespoons melted margarine
2 tablespoons chopped onion
1/4 cup chopped celery
1/2 teaspoon poultry seasoning
1 teaspoon salt

1/2 teaspoon pepper
5 cups chopped cooked chicken
3/4 cup all-purpose flour
1/2 cup melted margarine
4 cups chicken broth
6 eggs, slightly beaten
1 cup dry bread crumbs
2 teaspoons melted margarine

Preheat oven to 325 degrees. Combine bread cubes, evaporated milk, 3 tablespoons melted margarine, onion, celery, poultry seasoning, salt and pepper in bowl; mix well. Spread in greased 9x13-inch baking dish. Top with chicken. Blend flour into 1/2 cup margarine in double boiler. Stir in chicken broth. Cook until thickened, stirring constantly. Stir a small amount of hot mixture into eggs; stir eggs into hot mixture. Spoon over chicken. Top with mixture of bread crumbs and 2 teaspoons margarine. Bake until bubbly and set. Yield: 12 servings.

Approx Per Serving: Cal 427; Prot 27 g; Carbo 32 g; Fiber 1 g;
  T Fat 21 g; 44% Calories from Fat; Chol 159 mg; Sod 911 mg.

Chicken with Peanut Sauce

2 tablespoons minced gingerroot
2 tablespoons minced garlic
2 tablespoons oil
1 cup chicken broth
1/2 cup dry cooking sherry
2 tablespoons reduced-sodium
  soy sauce
2 tablespoons vinegar

2 teaspoons sesame oil
1/3 cup plus 2 tablespoons
  peanut butter
8 ounces chopped cooked
  chicken
3 cups cooked vermicelli
2 tablespoons chopped green
  onions

Sauté gingerroot and garlic in 2 tablespoons oil in skillet for 30 seconds. Add chicken broth, cooking sherry, soy sauce, vinegar, sesame oil and peanut butter; mix well. Simmer for 3 minutes or until thickened, stirring constantly. Stir in chopped chicken. Cook until heated through. Serve over vermicelli. Top with green onions. Yield: 4 servings.

Approx Per Serving: Cal 545; Prot 31 g; Carbo 34 g; Fiber 4 g;
    T Fat 29 g; 50% Calories from Fat; Chol 51 mg; Sod 562 mg.

Glazed Cornish Hens

2 7-ounce packages
  herb-seasoned stuffing mix
1 cup chopped pecans
2 cups brown minute rice,
  cooked
1 cup chopped celery
1/2 cup chopped parsley

8 Cornish game hens
1/4 cup melted margarine
1 6-ounce can frozen apple
  juice concentrate
1 tablespoon honey
1 tablespoon Dijon mustard

Preheat oven to 375 degrees. Prepare stuffing mix using package directions. Combine stuffing, pecans, rice, celery and parsley in bowl; mix well. Rinse hens inside and out; pat dry. Spoon stuffing into hens; secure with skewers. Spoon remaining stuffing into 1-quart baking dish. Place hens in roasting pan; brush with margarine. Place hens and additional stuffing in oven. Bake for 45 minutes or until drumstick moves easily, basting with pan juices several times. Heat apple juice concentrate in saucepan. Add honey and mustard; mix well. Place hens on serving plate. Mound additional baked stuffing in center. Spoon apple glaze over top. Yield: 8 servings.

Approx Per Serving: Cal 982; Prot 77 g; Carbo 86 g; Fiber 3 g;
    T Fat 36 g; 33% Calories from Fat; Chol 202 mg; Sod 996 mg.

Orange-Ginger Glazed Cornish Game Hen

1 1¹/₂-pound Cornish game hen, skinned
¹/₄ teaspoon each sage and rosemary, crumbled
1 clove of garlic, crushed
1 teaspoon minced fresh ginger
¹/₄ teaspoon pepper

1 3-inch strip orange rind
1 tablespoon olive oil
¹/₄ cup orange juice
1 tablespoon honey
1 tablespoon red wine vinegar
2 teaspoons Dijon mustard
1 teaspoon grated orange rind

Preheat oven to 375 degrees. Rinse game hen; pat dry inside and out. Sprinkle cavity with sage, rosemary, garlic, half the ginger and half the pepper; place orange strip inside. Truss hen; place breast-side up in shallow roasting pan. Brush with olive oil; sprinkle with remaining pepper. Roast for 35 to 40 minutes or until hen is tender. Combine orange juice, honey, vinegar, mustard and remaining ginger in small saucepan; mix well. Bring to a boil; reduce heat to medium. Simmer for 5 minutes or until mixture is syrupy, stirring frequently. Split hen lengthwise; baste with syrup. Broil, skinned side up, 5 inches from heat source for 2 to 3 minutes or until golden brown. Sprinkle with grated orange rind. Yield: 2 servings.

Approx Per Serving: Cal 444; Prot 50 g; Carbo 14 g; Fiber <1 g;
T Fat 20 g; 41% Calories from Fat; Chol 152 mg; Sod 280 mg.

Roast Turkey with Pistachio Stuffing

¹/₄ cup chicken broth
1 cup water
³/₄ cup apricot nectar
1 7-ounce package herb-seasoned stuffing mix

1 cup pistachios
1 cup chopped onion
¹/₂ cup chopped dried apricots
¹/₂ cup chopped dates
1 12-pound turkey

Preheat oven to 325 degrees. Combine chicken broth, water and apricot nectar in bowl. Stir in stuffing mix. Add pistachios, onion, apricots and dates; mix well. Stuff and truss turkey. Place in roasting pan. Roast for 3 to 4 hours or to 180 degrees on meat thermometer. Let stand for 15 minutes before carving. Yield: 10 servings.

Approx Per Serving: Cal 720; Prot 92 g; Carbo 36 g; Fiber 3 g;
T Fat 22 g; 28% Calories from Fat; Chol 225 mg; Sod 495 mg.

For a tomato rose, cut peel gently from a firm tomato in a continuous ¹/₂-inch strip with a sharp knife. Shape peel into a rose, starting at base end and placing skin side out. Add fresh herb leaves such as basil to resemble rose leaves.

Grilled Turkey Breast

¾ cup red cooking sherry
¼ cup light soy sauce
½ teaspoon garlic powder

½ teaspoon crushed basil
1 tablespoon olive oil
1 pound turkey scallops

Combine cooking sherry, soy sauce, garlic powder, basil and oil in shallow bowl; mix well. Rinse turkey and pat dry. Marinate turkey in sauce in refrigerator. Drain, reserving marinade. Grill turkey over hot coals for 10 minutes or until tender, basting occasionally with reserved marinade. Yield: 4 servings.

Approx Per Serving: Cal 222; Prot 26 g; Carbo 2 g; Fiber 0 g;
    T Fat 6 g; 25% Calories from Fat; Chol 59 mg; Sod 448 mg.

Turkey and Pears Sauté

1 pound turkey breast slices
2 cloves of garlic, chopped
2 tablespoons olive oil
1 teaspoon cracked peppercorns
⅓ cup apple juice

2 tablespoons evaporated skim
    milk
2 pears, sliced ¼ inch thick
½ cup pecan halves, toasted
4 cups cooked rice

Rinse turkey and pat dry. Sauté turkey and garlic in hot oil in skillet for 1 to 2 minutes or until turkey is brown; reduce heat. Stir in peppercorns, apple juice, evaporated milk and pears. Cook for 1 to 2 minutes or until heated through. Arrange on serving platter. Sprinkle with toasted pecans. Serve over rice. Yield: 4 servings.

Approx Per Serving: Cal 573; Prot 32 g; Carbo 68 g; Fiber 4 g;
    T Fat 19 g; 30% Calories from Fat; Chol 59 mg; Sod 65 mg.

Barbecued Turkey

2 tablespoons minced onion
1 green bell pepper, chopped
¼ cup margarine
⅛ teaspoon Tabasco sauce
2 cups catsup
⅔ cup chicken broth

⅓ cup vinegar
⅓ cup sugar
⅓ teaspoon reduced-sodium
    Worcestershire sauce
5 cups chopped cooked turkey

Sauté onion and green pepper in margarine in saucepan. Add Tabasco sauce, catsup, broth, vinegar, sugar and Worcestershire sauce; mix well. Simmer for 10 minutes, stirring occasionally. Add turkey. Simmer for 20 minutes longer. May freeze and reheat in double boiler. Yield: 8 servings.

Approx Per Serving: Cal 312; Prot 28 g; Carbo 27 g; Fiber 1 g;
    T Fat 11 g; 30% Calories from Fat; Chol 67 mg; Sod 906 mg.

Exotic Curried Turkey

3 tablespoons chopped onion
3 tablespoons chopped apple
3 tablespoons chopped celery
1/4 cup margarine
1/2 teaspoon each pepper, sugar
    and MSG
1/4 teaspoon nutmeg
21/2 teaspoons curry powder
1 teaspoon salt

1/4 cup all-purpose flour
11/2 cups low-fat milk
2 teaspoons lemon juice
3/4 teaspoon reduced-sodium
    Worcestershire sauce
3 cups chopped cooked turkey
6 cups cooked rice
1/2 cup raisins
1/2 cup sliced almonds

Brown onion, apple and celery in margarine in skillet. Add pepper, sugar, MSG, nutmeg, curry powder, salt and flour; mix well. Stir in milk. Cook over low heat until thickened, stirring constantly. Add lemon juice, Worcestershire sauce and turkey. Cook until heated through. Serve over mixture of rice, raisins and almonds. Garnish with chopped tomatoes, peanuts, coconut, chopped eggs and/or chopped green pepper. Yield: 6 servings.

Approx Per Serving: Cal 554; Prot 30 g; Carbo 71 g; Fiber 3 g;
    T Fat 17 g; 27% Calories from Fat; Chol 59 mg; Sod 533 mg.

Turkey-Sauced Pasta

1 cup sliced celery
1 small onion, chopped
1 cup sliced carrots
1/2 teaspoon basil
3/4 cup water

1 cup nonfat yogurt
1   7-ounce can reduced-sodium
    cream of mushroom soup
2 cups chopped cooked turkey
8 cups hot cooked noodles

Bring celery, onion, carrots, basil and water to a boil in saucepan; reduce heat. Simmer, covered, for 5 to 7 minutes. Add yogurt, soup and turkey; mix well. Cook until heated through, stirring occasionally. Serve over noodles. Yield: 4 servings.

Approx Per Serving: Cal 607; Prot 38 g; Carbo 86 g; Fiber 9 g;
    T Fat 10 g; 15% Calories from Fat; Chol 154 mg; Sod 142 mg.

Turkey Tetrazzini

1/4 cup margarine
1 4-ounce can sliced
   mushrooms, drained
1 small onion, chopped
1 1/2 teaspoons lemon juice
1/3 cup all-purpose flour
1 teaspoon salt
1/2 teaspoon paprika

1/8 teaspoon nutmeg
2 cups turkey broth
1/2 cup evaporated skim milk
2 1/2 cups chopped cooked turkey
7 ounces spaghetti, cooked
1/2 cup grated Parmesan cheese
Paprika to taste

Combine margarine, mushrooms, onion and lemon juice in 2-quart microwave-safe casserole. Microwave on High for 2 to 3 minutes or until tender, stirring after 1 minute. Stir in flour, salt, 1/2 teaspoon paprika and nutmeg until smooth. Microwave for 1 minute. Add broth. Microwave for 6 to 8 minutes or until thickened, stirring after 3 minutes. Add evaporated milk and turkey; mix well. Place cooked spaghetti in greased 8x12-inch baking dish. Add turkey mixture. Sprinkle with cheese and paprika to taste. Microwave for 7 minutes or until heated through. Yield: 4 servings.

Approx Per Serving: Cal 580; Prot 43 g; Carbo 54 g; Fiber 4 g;
     T Fat 20 g; 32% Calories from Fat; Chol 77 mg; Sod 1464 mg.

Turkey Tortellini

2 10-ounce cans cream of
   asparagus soup
1 pound fresh asparagus,
   trimmed, sliced
3 cups chopped cooked turkey
2 teaspoons poultry seasoning

1 tablespoon lemon juice
4 ounces shredded sharp
   Cheddar cheese
1 1/4 pounds cheese tortellini,
   cooked

Combine soup, asparagus, turkey, seasoning and lemon juice in large saucepan; mix well. Simmer for 20 minutes or until asparagus is tender, stirring frequently. Stir in cheese just before serving. Pour over cooked tortellini. Yield: 6 servings.

Approx Per Serving: Cal 572; Prot 44 g; Carbo 56 g; Fiber 2 g;
     T Fat 20 g; 31% Calories from Fat; Chol 122 mg; Sod 517 mg.

Seafood

Swiss Filet Rolls

1 pound whitefish filets
Salt and pepper to taste
2 cups sliced fresh mushrooms
1/2 cup chopped onion
2 tablespoons margarine
1 cup herb-seasoned stuffing mix

1 tablespoon margarine
1 tablespoon all-purpose flour
Salt to taste
1/2 cup lowfat milk
1/4 cup shredded Swiss cheese

Sprinkle fish with salt and pepper. Combine mushrooms, onion, and 2 tablespoons margarine in glass dish. Microwave on High for 2 to 3 minutes or until margarine is melted. Stir in stuffing mix. Spread over fish; roll up. Place seam side down in glass baking dish. Cover with vented plastic wrap. Microwave on High for 4 to 4 1/2 minutes or until fish flakes easily. Set aside. Microwave remaining 1 tablespoon margarine in glass bowl until melted. Stir in flour, salt and milk. Microwave on High for 1 to 1 1/2 minutes or until boiling and thickened, stirring once. Stir in cheese. Spoon over fish rolls. Garnish with parsley. Yield: 4 servings.

Approx Per Serving: Cal 315; Prot 28 g; Carbo 19 g; Fiber 1 g;
    T Fat 14 g; 40% Calories from Fat; Chol 73 mg; Sod 461 mg.

Dress up party vegetables by tying bundles of green beans, asparagus or julienne carrots with chives. Decorate party platters with wedges of baked sweet potato or thin wedges of baked acorn squash.

Fish Lovers' Delight

1 pound whitefish filets, cut into
  pieces
1/2 lemon
6 ounces fresh mushrooms, sliced
6 to 8 scallions, chopped
Garlic salt and basil to taste

1 16-ounce can whole tomatoes,
  drained, chopped
2 tablespoons melted margarine
1/4 cup bread crumbs
2 tablespoons grated Parmesan
  cheese

Preheat oven to 425 degrees. Arrange fish in single layer in 7x12-inch baking dish sprayed with nonstick cooking spray. Squeeze lemon juice over fish. Add mushrooms and scallions. Season with garlic salt and basil. Top with tomatoes. Pour margarine over tomatoes. Bake, covered, with foil, for 15 minutes. Sprinkle with bread crumbs and cheese. Broil for 1 to 2 minutes or until bread crumbs are golden brown. Yield: 6 servings.

Approx Per Serving: Cal 156; Prot 18 g; Carbo 9 g; Fiber 2 g;
    T Fat 6 g; 33% Calories from Fat; Chol 43 mg; Sod 295 mg.

Italian-Style Fish and Vegetables

2 tablespoons oil
1 onion, cut into slices
1 3-ounce jar sliced
  mushrooms, drained
1/2 teaspoon basil leaves

2 cups frozen mixed vegetables
1 1/2 pounds orange roughy
1/4 teaspoon each salt and pepper
2 tomatoes, sliced
1/3 cup grated Parmesan cheese

Heat oil in skillet over medium heat. Add onion, mushrooms and basil. Sauté until onion is tender. Stir in vegetables. Top with fish. Sprinkle with salt and pepper. Arrange tomatoes over fish. Reduce temperature to low. Cook, covered, for 12 to 16 minutes or until fish flakes easily. Remove from heat. Sprinkle with cheese. Let stand, covered, for 3 minutes. Yield: 6 servings.

Approx Per Serving: Cal 222; Prot 26 g; Carbo 13 g; Fiber 4 g;
    T Fat 8 g; 30% Calories from Fat; Chol 65 mg; Sod 353 mg.

Shrimp-Topped Sole

2 pounds sole filets
1 4-ounce can small shrimp

3 ounces cream cheese, softened
1/2 cup shrimp cocktail sauce

Place filets in 7x12-inch glass baking dish. Drain shrimp. Mix shrimp, cream cheese and cocktail sauce in bowl. Spread over filets. Cover tightly with waxed paper. Microwave on High for 10 to 16 minutes or until fish flakes easily. Let stand, covered, for 5 minutes. Yield: 4 servings.

Approx Per Serving: Cal 352; Prot 53 g; Carbo 8 g; Fiber 0 g;
    T Fat 11 g; 29% Calories from Fat; Chol 196 mg; Sod 509 mg.

Snapper Filets in Nut Crust

2 pounds skinless snapper filets
1/4 cup all-purpose flour
1 cup whole wheat bread crumbs
1 cup chopped pecans

1 egg yolk
2 egg whites
2 tablespoons water
2 tablespoons vegetable oil

Preheat oven to 350 degrees. Cut fish into serving size portions. Dust with flour. Mix crumbs and pecans in shallow dish. Beat egg yolk, egg whites and water in bowl. Heat oil in skillet. Dip fish into egg wash; coat with crumb mixture. Add to hot oil. Cook for 2 minutes per side or until golden brown. Place fish on ovenproof platter. Bake for 5 minutes. Yield: 6 servings.

Approx Per Serving: Cal 427; Prot 38 g; Carbo 20 g; Fiber 2 g;
   T Fat 22 g; 46% Calories from Fat; Chol 93 mg; Sod 210 mg.

Colossal Clam Sauce

1 onion, chopped
4 stalks celery, chopped
2 tablespoons margarine
1 chicken bouillon cube
1 cup water
2   10-ounce cans reduced-sodium
    cream of mushroom soup

2 6-ounce cans chopped clams
1/2 teaspoon marjoram
1/2 teaspoon crushed rosemary
1/4 teaspoon garlic powder
1/4 teaspoon pepper
1/2 cup Parmesan cheese

Sauté onion and celery in margarine in skillet. Add bouillon cube and water. Bring to a simmer. Stir in soup, clams, seasonings and cheese. Cook until heated through. May add a small amount of milk for desired consistency. Serve over spaghetti, linguine or spinach noodles. Yield: 6 servings.

Approx Per Serving: Cal 174; Prot 9 g; Carbo 10 g; Fiber 1 g;
   T Fat 14 g; 62% Calories from Fat; Chol 41 mg; Sod 425 mg.

Crab Meat Fettucini

4 large tomatoes, peeled, seeded,
   coarsely chopped
1 clove of garlic, crushed
1 bunch fresh basil, chopped
2 tablespoons olive oil

Salt and pepper to taste
8 ounces crab meat, warmed
1   16-ounce package fettucini,
    cooked, drained

Drain tomatoes partially. Combine with garlic, basil, olive oil, salt, pepper and crab meat in bowl; mix well. Serve over hot fettucini. Garnish with grated Parmesan cheese and pepper. Yield: 6 servings.

Approx Per Serving: Cal 373; Prot 15 g; Carbo 61 g; Fiber 4 g;
   T Fat 6 g; 14% Calories from Fat; Chol 30 mg; Sod 87 mg.

Rainbow Crab Delight

3 tablespoons olive oil
1 tablespoon minced garlic
1 onion, cut into rings
1 tablespoon minced fresh
  coriander
2 serrano peppers, minced
1 cup broccoli flowerets

1 cup 2-inch carrot strips
1 zucchini, cut into 2-inch pieces
1 small red pepper, cut into
  1/2-inch strips
8 ounces crab meat, cut into
  2-inch pieces
Salt to taste

Heat oil in skillet. Add garlic and onion. Sauté just until heated through. Add coriander, serrano peppers, broccoli, carrots, zucchini and red pepper. Sauté for 5 to 6 minutes or until coated. Add crab meat; reduce temperature. Cook, covered, until vegetables are tender-crisp, stirring several times. Season with salt. Yield: 4 servings.

Approx Per Serving: Cal 202; Prot 14 g; Carbo 12 g; Fiber 3 g;
     T Fat 12 g; 50% Calories from Fat; Chol 57 mg; Sod 175 mg.

Haddock Bienville

1 1/2 pounds haddock
Salt and pepper to taste
1 egg, beaten
1/2 cup grated Cheddar cheese
2 tablespoons melted margarine
1 teaspoon reduced-sodium
  Worcestershire sauce

1 tablespoon lemon juice
2 tablespoons each chopped
  green onions and chopped
  parsley
1/2 cup sliced mushrooms
7 ounces cooked peeled shrimp

Arrange filets in single layer in 8x8-inch microwave-safe dish. Season with salt and pepper. Combine egg, cheese, margarine, Worcestershire sauce, lemon juice, green onions, parsley, mushrooms and shrimp in bowl; mix well. Spread over filets. Microwave, covered, on High for 8 minutes. Let stand, covered, for 2 minutes. Yield: 8 servings.

Approx Per Serving: Cal 170; Prot 26 g; Carbo 1 g; Fiber <1 g;
     T Fat 7 g; 36% Calories from Fat; Chol 133 mg; Sod 207 mg.

For radish mums, select round radishes. Trim off root ends and make several thin crosswise cuts almost to the bottom of the radish. Make additional cuts perpendicular to the first cuts. Chill in iced water until radish opens.

Savory Stuffed Flounder

2 12-inch whole flounder
1 package Stove-Top stuffing
1/2 cup chopped onion
1/2 cup chopped celery

2 tablespoons melted margarine
1/2 cup chopped crab meat
2 slices bacon
Salt and pepper to taste

Preheat broiler. Slit dark side of flounder to create pocket for stuffing. Place on broiler pan sprayed with nonstick cooking spray. Prepare stuffing using package directions. Sauté onion and celery in margarine in skillet. Stir into stuffing. Add crab meat; mix well. Stuff into flounder. Top with bacon. Season with salt and pepper. Broil for 20 to 30 minutes or until fish flakes easily. Yield: 4 servings.

Approx Per Serving: Cal 575; Prot 56 g; Carbo 33 g; Fiber 5 g;
T Fat 24 g; 37% Calories from Fat; Chol 179 mg; Sod 1328 mg.

Grouper with Citrus Rice

4 6-ounce grouper filets
2 tablespoons olive oil
1 large onion, chopped
1 tablespoon grated lemon rind

1 cup orange slices
4 teaspoons lemon juice
4 cups hot cooked rice

Preheat oven to 350 degrees. Place filets in shallow baking dish. Heat olive oil in skillet. Add onion. Sauté for 2 minutes or until clear and golden. Add lemon rind, orange slices and 2 teaspoons lemon juice. Cook for 1 minute longer; remove from heat. Spoon over filets. Sprinkle with remaining 2 teaspoons lemon juice. Bake, covered, for 15 to 20 minutes or until fish flakes easily. Flake fish; arrange over hot cooked rice. Yield: 4 servings.

Approx Per Serving: Cal 504; Prot 41 g; Carbo 57 g; Fiber 2 g;
T Fat 11 g; 20% Calories from Fat; Chol 56 mg; Sod 95 mg.

Gourmet Tuna and Spaghetti

8 ounces spaghetti, cooked
4 tablespoons margarine
1 clove of garlic, minced
2 tablespoons olive oil

1 cup chicken stock
3 tablespoons white grape juice
1 8-ounce can water-pack tuna
Salt and pepper to taste

Toss spaghetti with 2 tablespoons margarine. Sauté garlic in olive oil and 2 tablespoons margarine in skillet. Add chicken stock, grape juice and drained tuna. Bring to a boil. Simmer for several minutes. Add to spaghetti. Season with salt and pepper. Yield: 4 servings.

Approx Per Serving: Cal 463; Prot 25 g; Carbo 45 g; Fiber 3 g;
T Fat 20 g; 38% Calories from Fat; Chol 32 mg; Sod 531 mg.

Tuna-Pasta Bake

6 uncooked lasagna noodles
1/2 cup chopped onion
1 tablespoon oil
1/4 cup all-purpose flour
2 cups frozen mixed vegetables
1 cup low-fat milk
1/3 cup lemon juice

1 1/2 cups shredded mozzarella
 cheese
1 cup low-fat cottage cheese
1/4 cup grated Parmesan cheese
1 egg
1 12-ounce can water-pack tuna,
 drained

Place noodles and water to cover in 7x12-inch glass dish. Combine onion, oil and flour in glass bowl; mix well. Microwave on High for 1 minute. Stir in vegetables and milk. Microwave for 4 minutes longer, stirring once. Add lemon juice; mix well. Mix cheeses, egg and tuna in bowl. Drain noodles. Layer vegetable mixture and tuna mixture over noodles. Microwave on High for 15 minutes. Yield: 9 servings.

Approx Per Serving: Cal 284; Prot 25 g; Carbo 26 g; Fiber 2 g;
     T Fat 8 g; 27% Calories from Fat; Chol 66 mg; Sod 386 mg.

Tuna Shells Neapolitan

1 10-ounce can reduced-sodium
 cream of celery soup
1/2 teaspoon lemon juice
1/4 teaspoon crushed oregano
1 10-ounce package frozen
 chopped broccoli, cooked,
 drained

1/2 cup chopped drained canned
 tomatoes
1 7-ounce can water-pack tuna,
 drained, flaked
24 jumbo macaroni shells,
 cooked, drained
1/2 cup shredded Cheddar cheese

Preheat oven to 400 degrees. Mix celery soup, lemon juice, oregano, broccoli, tomatoes and tuna in bowl. Spoon 1/4 cup mixture into each macaroni shell. Arrange in 6x10-inch baking dish. Bake for 20 minutes or until heated through. Sprinkle with cheese. Bake for 5 minutes longer or until cheese is melted. Garnish with parsley. Yield: 12 servings.

Approx Per Serving: Cal 136; Prot 10 g; Carbo 18 g; Fiber 2 g;
     T Fat 3 g; 20% Calories from Fat; Chol 17 mg; Sod 289 mg.

Chill butter in individual butter or candy molds to make servings in holiday shapes. To make butter curls, dip the blade of a vegetable peeler into hot water and pull it firmly over a slightly softened stick of butter. Chill the curls in iced water.

Scallops and Pasta

8 ounces scallops
8 ounces mushrooms, sliced
1 small onion, chopped
1/2 cup chopped green bell pepper
1 tablespoon margarine
1 tablespoon oil

1/8 teaspoon each nutmeg, salt
  and pepper
1 cup plain nonfat yogurt
1/4 cup grated Parmesan cheese
8 ounces spaghetti, cooked,
  drained

Sauté scallops, mushrooms, onion and green pepper in margarine and oil in skillet for 5 minutes or until scallops are cooked through and vegetables are tender. Stir in nutmeg, salt, pepper, yogurt and cheese. Spoon over spaghetti. Yield: 4 servings.

Approx Per Serving: Cal 388; Prot 24 g; Carbo 52 g; Fiber 4 g;
  T Fat 9 g; 22% Calories from Fat; Chol 25 mg; Sod 264 mg.

Curried Shrimp

2 tablespoons chopped onion
1 tablespoon margarine
1 1/2 teaspoons curry powder
1   10-ounce can cream of celery
  soup

3/4 pound cooked shrimp
1/3 cup light sour cream
1 apple, peeled, chopped
3 cups cooked minute rice
2 tablespoons chopped parsley

Sauté onion in margarine in saucepan until transparent. Stir in curry powder, soup and shrimp. Cook until bubbly. Reduce heat. Add sour cream and apple; mix well. Cook until heated through; do not boil. Pour over hot cooked rice. Sprinkle with parsley. Serve with chutney. Yield: 4 servings.

Approx Per Serving: Cal 342; Prot 22 g; Carbo 41 g; Fiber 2 g;
  T Fat 10 g; 25% Calories from Fat; Chol 182 mg; Sod 769 mg.

Shrimp in Olive Sauce

1/2 cup chopped onion
1/4 cup melted margarine
2 tablespoons all-purpose flour
1 cup chicken broth
1/2 cup white grape juice
1/2 cup chopped parsley

1 tablespoon reduced-sodium
  soy sauce
1/2 cup stuffed olives
8 ounces cooked shrimp
1 cup sliced mushrooms
4 cups cooked rice

Sauté onion in margarine in skillet until tender. Add next 6 ingredients; mix well. Stir in shrimp and mushrooms. Cook until heated through. Serve over hot cooked rice. Yield: 4 servings.

Approx Per Serving: Cal 452; Prot 19 g; Carbo 61 g; Fiber 2 g;
  T Fat 14 g; 29% Calories from Fat; Chol 111 mg; Sod 813 mg.

Shrimp Étouffée

2 pounds shrimp, peeled, boiled
Salt, black pepper and red
   pepper to taste
1/2 cup margarine
1 cup chopped onion
1/2 cup chopped green bell
   pepper
1/4 teaspoon garlic salt

1 10-ounce can reduced-sodium
   cream of mushroom soup
1 10-ounce can cream of celery
   soup
1 10-ounce can reduced-sodium
   tomato soup
6 cups cooked rice

Season shrimp with salt, black pepper and red pepper. Melt margarine in nonstick 10-inch skillet. Add onion, green pepper and garlic salt. Cook over low heat until onion is wilted. Stir in shrimp. Simmer for 20 minutes. Add soups; mix well. Cook for 1 minute longer. Serve over hot cooked rice. Yield: 6 servings.

Approx Per Serving: Cal 594; Prot 32 g; Carbo 65 g; Fiber 1 g;
     T Fat 22 g; 33% Calories from Fat; Chol 241 mg; Sod 1082 mg.

Scampi Primavera

1 10-ounce package spaghetti
3/4 cup olive oil
3 large cloves of garlic, minced
1/2 teaspoon finely chopped
   lemon rind
2 carrots, julienned
1 zucchini, julienned
1 red pepper, julienned

1 1/2 pounds medium shrimp,
   peeled, deveined
2 tablespoons lemon juice
3/4 teaspoon salt
1/8 teaspoon black pepper
2 teaspoons dried parsley
2 teaspoons dried basil

Cook spaghetti using package directions; drain. Heat oil in large skillet. Add garlic and lemon rind. Cook for 30 seconds, stirring constantly. Add carrots, zucchini, red pepper and shrimp; mix well. Cook over medium heat for 3 to 4 minutes or until shrimp turn pink, stirring frequently. Sprinkle with lemon juice, salt and black pepper. Stir in parsley and basil. Spoon over spaghetti; toss well. Yield: 8 servings.

Approx Per Serving: Cal 395; Prot 19 g; Carbo 31 g; Fiber 3 g;
     T Fat 22 g; 49% Calories from Fat; Chol 133 mg; Sod 361 mg.

Make kumquat flowers by cutting canned or fresh kumquats into 6 wedges, cutting to but not through bottom to make petals.

Shrimp and Rice with Salsa

1 family size boil-in-bag rice
1 small onion, coarsely chopped
1 small green bell pepper,
  coarsely chopped
1 8-ounce can tomato sauce

1/3 cup picante sauce
1 tablespoon lime juice
1 pound medium shrimp,
  peeled, deveined
1/4 cup coarsely chopped cilantro

Cook rice using package directions. Combine onion and green pepper in large skillet sprayed with nonstick cooking spray. Cook for 2 minutes, stirring frequently. Stir in tomato sauce, picante sauce and lime juice. Bring to a boil. Simmer for 10 minutes. Stir in shrimp. Cook, covered, for 5 minutes or until shrimp turn pink. Spoon over hot cooked rice. Sprinkle with cilantro. Yield: 4 servings.

Approx Per Serving: Cal 220; Prot 22 g; Carbo 29 g; Fiber 2 g;
  T Fat 1 g; 6% Calories from Fat; Chol 177 mg; Sod 664 mg.

Seafood au Gratin

6 tablespoons margarine
1/2 cup all-purpose flour
2 cups low-fat milk
8 ounces shredded Cheddar
  cheese
6 ounces Monterey Jack cheese,
  cubed
1 12-ounce package frozen
  salad shrimp, thawed, drained

1 6-ounce can crab meat, drained
8 ounces fresh sea scallops, cut
  into halves
1 teaspoon thyme
1 teaspoon parsley flakes
1/2 teaspoon dry mustard
1/2 teaspoon garlic salt
Salt and pepper to taste
1/2 cup grated Parmesan cheese

Preheat broiler. Melt margarine in 6-quart saucepan. Stir in flour and milk. Cook until smooth and thickened, stirring frequently. Add Cheddar and Monterey Jack cheeses. Cook until melted, stirring constantly. Add shrimp, crab meat and scallops gradually. Stir in seasonings. Cook for 10 to 15 minutes or until heated through, stirring frequently. Spoon into individual shells or baking dishes. Sprinkle with Parmesan cheese. Broil for 3 to 5 minutes or until bubbly. Yield: 8 servings.

Approx Per Serving: Cal 441; Prot 36 g; Carbo 10 g; Fiber <1 g;
  T Fat 28 g; 58% Calories from Fat; Chol 171 mg; Sod 854 mg.

For a party conversation piece, decorate a whole poached fish with a spread of herbed mayonnaise, black olive scales and a caper eye.

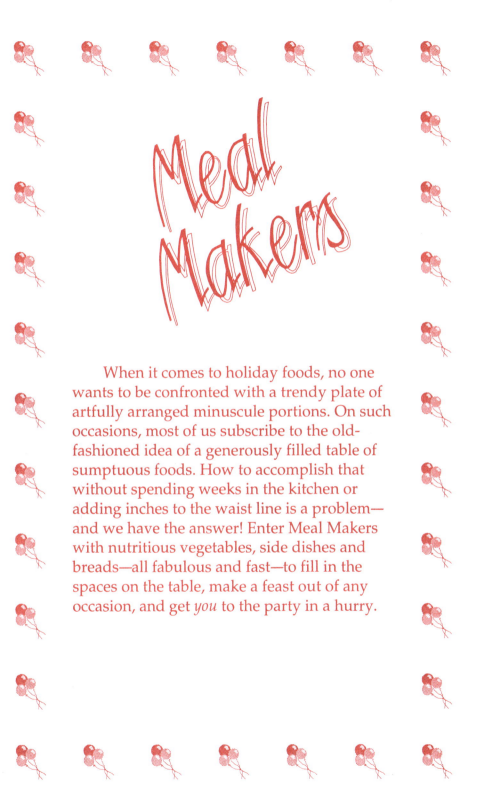

Meal Makers

When it comes to holiday foods, no one wants to be confronted with a trendy plate of artfully arranged minuscule portions. On such occasions, most of us subscribe to the old-fashioned idea of a generously filled table of sumptuous foods. How to accomplish that without spending weeks in the kitchen or adding inches to the waist line is a problem— and we have the answer! Enter Meal Makers with nutritious vegetables, side dishes and breads—all fabulous and fast—to fill in the spaces on the table, make a feast out of any occasion, and get *you* to the party in a hurry.

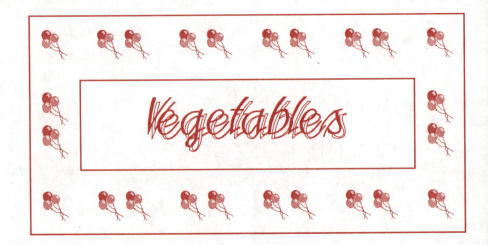

Vegetables

Artichoke and Spinach Soufflés

1 16-ounce can artichoke
   bottoms
1 package frozen spinach
   soufflé, thawed

1 cup light sour cream
1 lemon
1 hard-cooked egg, chopped

Preheat oven to 375 degrees. Rinse and drain artichoke bottoms; place on baking sheet. Place 1 scoop of spinach soufflé on each artichoke. Bake for 10 minutes or until soufflé is puffy and golden brown. Place a dollop of sour cream on each; drizzle with lemon juice. Sprinkle chopped egg over top; spoon onto serving plate. Yield: 6 servings.

Approx Per Serving: Cal 188; Prot 8 g; Carbo 8 g; Fiber 2 g;
     T Fat 14 g; 66% Calories from Fat; Chol 128 mg; Sod 534 mg.

Gingered Asparagus

1 pound fresh mushrooms
1 pound fresh asparagus
8 thin slices fresh gingerroot

1/4 cup oil
Salt and pepper to taste
1/4 teaspoon sugar

Slice mushrooms. Cut asparagus into diagonal slices. Chop gingerroot. Stir-fry asparagus and gingerroot in oil in wok or skillet over medium heat for 1 minute. Sprinkle with salt. Add mushrooms, pepper and sugar. Stir-fry for 1 minute longer. Yield: 4 servings.

Approx Per Serving: Cal 178; Prot 6 g; Carbo 10 g; Fiber 4 g;
     T Fat 14 g; 67% Calories from Fat; Chol 0 mg; Sod 7 mg.

Barbecued Black Beans

2 16-ounce cans black beans, drained
1 14-ounce can stewed tomatoes
1 11-ounce can vacuum-packed corn or 1 10-ounce package frozen corn

1 4-ounce can chopped green chilies
2 tablespoons barbecue sauce
3/4 teaspoon ground cumin
Salt and pepper to taste
4 cups cooked rice

Combine beans, tomatoes, corn, green chilies, barbecue sauce, cumin, salt and pepper in saucepan. Simmer for 10 minutes, stirring occasionally. Serve over hot cooked rice. Yield: 8 servings.

Approx Per Serving: Cal 267; Prot 11 g; Carbo 56 g; Fiber 1 g; T Fat 1 g; 2% Calories from Fat; Chol 0 mg; Sod 834 mg.

Lemony Green Beans

2 cups frozen cut green beans
1 cup water
1/4 cup sliced almonds
2 tablespoons melted margarine

2 teaspoons lemon juice
1 teaspoon grated lemon rind
1/4 teaspoon salt

Cook green beans in water in saucepan until tender-crisp; drain. Spoon into serving dish; keep warm. Sauté almonds in margarine in skillet for 2 minutes. Add lemon juice, lemon rind and salt; mix well. Spoon over green beans. Yield: 4 servings.

Approx Per Serving: Cal 104; Prot 2 g; Carbo 6 g; Fiber 3 g; T Fat 9 g; 72% Calories from Fat; Chol 0 mg; Sod 209 mg.

Spanish Bean Casserole

1 16-ounce can kidney beans
1 16-ounce can garbanzo beans
1 16-ounce can black beans
1 medium onion, chopped
2 tablespoons oil
2 cups uncooked long grain rice
1 16-ounce can stewed tomatoes

1 4-ounce can chopped green chilies, drained
3 cups water
1 10-ounce package frozen peas, thawed
1/2 cup pimento-stuffed green olives

Preheat oven to 375 degrees. Rinse and drain beans. Sauté onion in oil in Dutch oven until tender. Add rice. Cook until opaque. Add beans, tomatoes, green chilies and water. Bring to a boil. Bake, covered, for 30 minutes. Stir in peas and olives. Bake for 15 minutes longer. Yield: 12 servings.

Approx Per Serving: Cal 282; Prot 10 g; Carbo 53 g; Fiber 5 g; T Fat 4 g; 12% Calories from Fat; Chol 0 mg; Sod 691 mg.

Broccoli with Almonds

Flowerets of 2 pounds fresh
 broccoli
¼ cup sliced almonds

¼ cup margarine
Salt and pepper to taste

Cook broccoli in 1 inch boiling water in saucepan for 10 minutes; drain. Place in serving bowl. Sauté almonds in margarine in skillet until golden brown. Spoon onto broccoli. Add salt and pepper to taste. Yield: 6 servings.

Approx Per Serving: Cal 132; Prot 5 g; Carbo 9 g; Fiber 5 g;
 T Fat 10 g; 62% Calories from Fat; Chol 0 mg; Sod 131 mg.

Zippy Broccoli

3 egg yolks
3 tablespoons vinegar
¾ cup cold water
2 tablespoons sugar
1 tablespoon cornstarch

¾ teaspoon salt
2 tablespoons prepared
 horseradish
Flowerets of 1 large bunch
 broccoli

Process egg yolks, vinegar, water, sugar, cornstarch and salt in blender until smooth. Pour into double boiler. Cook until thickened, stirring constantly; remove from heat. Stir in horseradish. Chill in refrigerator. Cook broccoli in boiling water in saucepan just until tender-crisp but still bright green. Rinse and drain. Chill in refrigerator. Arrange broccoli on serving platter. Spoon horseradish sauce over broccoli. Garnish with grated radishes or red bell pepper strips. Yield: 8 servings.

Approx Per Serving: Cal 54; Prot 2 g; Carbo 7 g; Fiber 1 g;
 T Fat 2 g; 35% Calories from Fat; Chol 80 mg; Sod 218 mg.

Broccoli with Oranges

2 pounds fresh broccoli
2 tablespoons margarine
2 tablespoons all-purpose flour
1 cup orange juice

1 teaspoon grated orange rind
¼ teaspoon tarragon
½ cup nonfat yogurt
1 cup orange sections

Trim broccoli; separate into spears. Cook in a small amount of water in saucepan until tender-crisp. Melt margarine in heavy saucepan over low heat. Blend in flour. Cook for 1 minute, stirring constantly. Add orange juice. Cook until thickened, stirring constantly. Stir in orange rind and tarragon; remove from heat. Stir in yogurt. Drain broccoli. Arrange on serving plate. Spoon sauce over top. Top with orange sections. Yield: 10 servings.

Approx Per Serving: Cal 77; Prot 4 g; Carbo 12 g; Fiber 4 g;
 T Fat 3 g; 28% Calories from Fat; Chol <1 mg; Sod 60 mg.

West Coast Cauliflower

1 medium head cauliflower
1/4 cup water
8 ounces onion or garlic-flavored
  chip-style dip

8 ounces Cheddar cheese,
  shredded
1 teaspoon salad seasonings

Discard outer leaves of cauliflower. Wash cauliflower; place in microwave-safe dish. Add water. Microwave, tightly covered with plastic wrap, on High for 10 to 12 minutes or until tender-crisp, turning once. Drain excess liquid. Spread dip over cauliflower; sprinkle with cheese and salad seasonings. Broil until cheese is melted. Cut into wedges. Yield: 8 servings.

Approx Per Serving: Cal 175; Prot 9 g; Carbo 6 g; Fiber 1 g;
  T Fat 13 g; 67% Calories from Fat; Chol 30 mg; Sod 384 mg.

Velvet Corn Pudding

1 cup egg substitute
6 tablespoons melted margarine
3 tablespoons all-purpose flour
1/2 teaspoon onion powder
1/4 teaspoon red pepper
1/4 teaspoon garlic powder

1/2 teaspoon salt
1   10-ounce package frozen
  whole kernel corn
1   17-ounce can cream-style corn
1 cup evaporated skim milk

Preheat oven to 325 degrees. Combine egg substitute and margarine in mixer bowl. Add flour, onion powder, red pepper, garlic powder and salt; beat until smooth. Stir in whole kernel corn, cream-style corn and evaporated milk. Spoon into greased deep 1 1/2-quart baking dish. Bake for 1 1/2 hours or until knife inserted near center comes out clean. Let stand for 5 minutes. Yield: 10 servings.

Approx Per Serving: Cal 169; Prot 7 g; Carbo 20 g; Fiber 2 g;
  T Fat 8 g; 40% Calories from Fat; Chol 1 mg; Sod 399 mg.

Honey-Baked Onions

6 medium yellow onions
1/4 cup honey

2 tablespoons margarine
2 tablespoons chopped parsley

Peel onions and cut into halves crosswise. Arrange in 7x11-inch glass dish. Pour honey over top. Dot with margarine. Microwave, loosely covered with waxed paper, on High for 8 to 10 minutes or until tender, basting with pan juices twice. Sprinkle with parsley. Let stand for 3 minutes. Yield: 12 servings.

Approx Per Serving: Cal 66; Prot 1 g; Carbo 12 g; Fiber 1 g;
  T Fat 2 g; 27% Calories from Fat; Chol 0 mg; Sod 25 mg.

Baked Potato Fans

4 medium baking potatoes
1 teaspoon salt
3 tablespoons melted margarine
2 to 3 teaspoons chopped fresh
   parsley, chives, thyme or dill

1/4 cup shredded Cheddar cheese
1 1/2 tablespoons grated
   Parmesan cheese

Preheat oven to 425 degrees. Cut potatoes into thin slices, cutting to but not through bottom. Place in baking pan. Sprinkle with salt; drizzle with margarine. Sprinkle with choice of herbs. Bake for 50 minutes or until tender. Sprinkle with cheeses. Bake until cheeses melt. Yield: 4 servings.

Approx Per Serving: Cal 334; Prot 7 g; Carbo 51 g; Fiber 5 g;
   T Fat 12 g; 31% Calories from Fat; Chol 9 mg; Sod 729 mg.

Barbecued Potatoes

2 large potatoes
1 tablespoon melted margarine
1 tablespoon honey

2 teaspoons chili powder
1/8 teaspoon pepper
1/4 teaspoon garlic powder

Preheat oven to 425 degrees. Cut potatoes into thin slices; place in baking pan sprayed with nonstick cooking spray. Combine margarine, honey, chili powder, pepper and garlic powder in bowl; mix well. Spread evenly over potatoes. Bake for 15 to 20 minutes or until tender. Yield: 4 servings.

Approx Per Serving: Cal 152; Prot 2 g; Carbo 30 g; Fiber 2 g;
   T Fat 3 g; 17% Calories from Fat; Chol 0 mg; Sod 42 mg.

Chantilly Stuffed Potatoes

5 large baking potatoes
1 cup low-fat cottage cheese
1/2 cup shredded mozzarella
   cheese

1/4 cup Parmesan cheese
Salt and pepper to taste
Paprika to taste

Preheat oven to 350 degrees. Bake potatoes for 1 hour or until tender. Cut potatoes into halves lengthwise. Scoop pulp into bowl, reserving shells. Add cheeses, salt and pepper; beat until smooth. Spoon into potato shells. Place on baking sheet. Sprinkle with paprika. Bake for 10 minutes or until heated through. Yield: 10 servings.

Approx Per Serving: Cal 156; Prot 7 g; Carbo 27 g; Fiber 2 g;
   T Fat 2 g; 13% Calories from Fat; Chol 8 mg; Sod 159 mg.

Caesar Scalloped Potatoes

1 medium onion, chopped
2 large cloves of garlic, minced
1¹/₂ tablespoons margarine
1 tablespoon all-purpose flour
1 cup low-fat milk

¹/₃ cup grated Parmesan cheese
2 cups cubed potatoes
1 teaspoon Dijon mustard
¹/₂ teaspoon pepper
¹/₂ teaspoon Worcestershire sauce

Combine onion, garlic and margarine in 4-cup microwave-safe casserole. Microwave on High for 1 to 2 minutes or until onion is tender. Stir in flour. Microwave on High for 30 seconds. Whisk in milk. Microwave on High for 2 to 4 minutes or until mixture boils and thickens slightly, stirring twice. Stir in remaining ingredients. Microwave, covered, on High for 6 minutes or until potatoes are tender, stirring twice. Yield: 4 servings.

Approx Per Serving: Cal 183; Prot 7 g; Carbo 22 g; Fiber 2 g;
   T Fat 8 g; 38% Calories from Fat; Chol 11 mg; Sod 250 mg.

Stuffed Potatoes Florentine

4 large potatoes
2 tablespoons olive oil
2 teaspoons corn oil
1   10-ounce package frozen
   chopped spinach, thawed

2 cloves of garlic, minced
¹/₃ cup plain nonfat yogurt
1 cup whole wheat bread crumbs
4 teaspoons melted margarine

Preheat oven to 400 degrees. Microwave potatoes on High for 10 to 15 minutes or until tender. Cut into quarters; scoop out pulp and reserve. Mix olive oil and corn oil in bowl. Brush both sides of potato skins with oil; place cut side up on baking sheet. Bake for 10 minutes. Reduce oven temperature to 350 degrees. Heat remaining oil in skillet. Add spinach and garlic. Cook until most of moisture evaporates, stirring frequently. Remove from heat. Combine potato pulp and yogurt in mixer bowl; beat until smooth. Add spinach and half the bread crumbs; mix well. Combine remaining bread crumbs and melted margarine in bowl, tossing to mix. Mound potato mixture into potato skins; sprinkle with bread crumb mixture. Place on baking sheet. Bake at 350 degrees for 10 minutes or until light brown. May be frozen before baking. Yield: 6 servings.

Approx Per Serving: Cal 304; Prot 8 g; Carbo 49 g; Fiber 5 g;
   T Fat 10 g; 28% Calories from Fat; Chol 1 mg; Sod 213 mg.

Mini Pumpkins with Peas and Onions

10 miniature pumpkins, rinsed,
dried

6 cups frozen peas with pearl
onions, cooked

Preheat oven to 425 degrees. Cut two 1-inch slits in sides of each pumpkin. Place in baking pan. Bake for 30 to 40 minutes or until tender. Cut slice from top of each pumpkin. Scoop out seed. Spoon peas and onions into pumpkins. Arrange on serving plate. Yield: 10 servings.

Approx Per Serving: Cal 110; Prot 7 g; Carbo 22 g; Fiber 2 g;
T Fat <1 g; 2% Calories from Fat; Chol 0 mg; Sod 376 mg.

Deluxe Spinach

2 10-ounce packages frozen
spinach, thawed

1 cup light sour cream
1 envelope onion soup mix

Preheat oven to 350 degrees. Drain spinach, squeezing out excess moisture. Combine spinach, sour cream and onion soup mix in bowl; mix well. Pour into casserole. Bake at 350 degrees for 30 minutes. Yield: 8 servings.

Approx Per Serving: Cal 62; Prot 3 g; Carbo 6 g; Fiber 2 g;
T Fat 4 g; 50% Calories from Fat; Chol 12 mg; Sod 151 mg.

Spinach Soufflé Pie

1 package frozen spinach
soufflé, thawed
2 eggs, beaten
3 tablespoons milk
2 teaspoons chopped onion

1/2 cup sliced mushrooms
3/4 cup cooked crumbled Italian
sausage
3/4 cup shredded Swiss cheese
1 unbaked 9-inch pie shell

Preheat oven to 400 degrees. Combine spinach soufflé, eggs, milk, onion, mushrooms, Italian sausage and cheese in bowl; mix well. Pour into unbaked pie shell. Bake for 25 to 30 minutes or until set. May bake mixture in casserole instead of pie shell. Yield: 6 servings.

Approx Per Serving: Cal 368; Prot 15 g; Carbo 16 g; Fiber 2 g;
T Fat 27 g; 66% Calories from Fat; Chol 171 mg; Sod 680 mg.

Acorn Squash with Apple Stuffing

3 large acorn squash
4 cups chopped peeled apples
2 cups raisins
2 cups chopped pecans

2/3 cup sugar
2 teaspoons lemon juice
1/2 teaspoon cinnamon
1/2 teaspoon nutmeg

Preheat oven to 350 degrees. Slice off tops of squash; discard seed. Combine apples, raisins, pecans, sugar, lemon juice, cinnamon and nutmeg in bowl; mix well. Spoon apple mixture into squash; replace tops. Place in baking pan. Bake for 1 1/2 hours or until squash can be easily pierced with toothpick. Remove tops. Cut each squash into 4 wedges. Yield: 12 servings.

Approx Per Serving: Cal 339; Prot 4 g; Carbo 58 g; Fiber 7 g;
T Fat 14 g; 34% Calories from Fat; Chol 0 mg; Sod 8 mg.

Country Squash Casserole

1 pound yellow squash, sliced
8 ounces zucchini, sliced
1 cup water
1/2 cup chopped onion
1/4 cup chopped green bell
pepper
3 tablespoons chopped green
onions
1 tablespoon margarine
1 cup herb-seasoned stuffing mix

3 tablespoons melted margarine
1   10-ounce can cream of
chicken soup
1   8-ounce can water chestnuts,
drained, chopped
1/2 cup plain low-fat yogurt
1/4 cup chopped pimento
1 large carrot, grated
1/2 teaspoon salt
1/4 teaspoon pepper

Preheat oven to 350 degrees. Bring squash, zucchini and water to a boil in saucepan; cover and reduce heat. Simmer for 8 minutes or until tender; drain. Sauté onion, green pepper and green onions in 1 tablespoon margarine in skillet until tender; set aside. Mix stuffing mix and 3 tablespoons margarine in large bowl. Reserve 1/3 cup mixture for topping. Add squash mixture, sautéed mixture, soup, water chestnuts, yogurt, pimento, carrot, salt and pepper to remaining stuffing mixture; mix well. Spoon into lightly greased 8x12-inch baking dish. Sprinkle with reserved stuffing. Bake for 30 minutes or until heated through. Yield: 8 servings.

Approx Per Serving: Cal 165; Prot 4 g; Carbo 19 g; Fiber 3 g;
T Fat 9 g; 45% Calories from Fat; Chol 4 mg; Sod 613 mg.

Squash Extravaganza

1 medium summer squash,
  chopped
1 medium crookneck squash,
  chopped
4 green onions, finely chopped
1 medium zucchini, chopped
Greek seasoning to taste

1/4 cup fresh basil, chopped
1/2 teaspoon salt
Pepper to taste
1/2 cup water
1   15-ounce can stewed tomatoes
8 mushrooms

Combine summer squash, crookneck squash, green onions, zucchini, seasonings and water in saucepan. Cook, covered, until tender-crisp. Add tomatoes and mushrooms. Cook until mushrooms are tender. Spoon into serving bowl. May substitute or add any kind of squash. Yield: 8 servings.

Approx Per Serving: Cal 43; Prot 2 g; Carbo 10 g; Fiber 2 g;
    T Fat <1 g; 6% Calories from Fat; Chol 0 mg; Sod 308 mg.

Yellow Crookneck Squash Patties

3 cups grated yellow crookneck
  squash
1 green bell pepper, grated
1 small onion, grated
1 egg, slightly beaten

1/2 teaspoon salt
1/4 teaspoon pepper
1/4 cup all-purpose flour
2 tablespoons oil

Combine squash, green pepper, onion, egg, salt, pepper and flour in bowl; mix well. Drop by tablespoonfuls into hot oil in skillet. Cook until brown on both sides. Yield: 4 servings.

Approx Per Serving: Cal 159; Prot 5 g; Carbo 17 g; Fiber 4 g;
    T Fat 9 g; 48% Calories from Fat; Chol 53 mg; Sod 288 mg.

Festive Sweet Potatoes

4 cups mashed sweet potatoes
1 cup skim milk
3/4 cup egg substitute
1 cup packed light brown sugar
1/2 cup melted margarine

1 teaspoon cinnamon
1/2 teaspoon nutmeg
1 teaspoon vanilla extract
1/2 cup chopped pecans
1 cup miniature marshmallows

Preheat oven to 350 degrees. Combine sweet potatoes, milk, egg substitute, brown sugar, margarine, spices and vanilla in bowl; mix well. Spoon into greased 2-quart casserole. Bake for 40 minutes. Sprinkle with pecans and marshmallows. Bake for 5 minutes. Yield: 10 servings.

Approx Per Serving: Cal 404; Prot 6 g; Carbo 65 g; Fiber 2 g;
    T Fat 14 g; 31% Calories from Fat; Chol 1 mg; Sod 187 mg.

Sweet Potatoes in Apple Shells

6 large red baking apples, cut
  into halves lengthwise, cored
1 cup packed light brown sugar
5 cups mashed cooked sweet
  potatoes

1/2 teaspoon cinnamon
6 tablespoons melted margarine
6 tablespoons evaporated skim
  milk
2 tablespoons melted margarine

Preheat oven to 400 degrees. Place apples in shallow baking dish. Sprinkle with half the brown sugar. Add a small amount of water. Bake for 10 to 20 minutes or until slightly tender. Scoop out pulp, leaving 1/2-inch shells. Combine apple pulp with next 4 ingredients in mixer bowl. Beat until fluffy. Spoon into apple shells. Place in shallow baking dish. Sprinkle with remaining brown sugar. Drizzle with remaining 2 tablespoons margarine. Bake for 30 minutes or until heated through. Yield: 12 servings.

Approx Per Serving: Cal 365; Prot 3 g; Carbo 72 g; Fiber 4 g;
    T Fat 8 g; 20% Calories from Fat; Chol <1 mg; Sod 127 mg.

Baked Tomato Wedges

2 tablespoons fine dry bread
  crumbs
1/4 cup each finely chopped
  onion and fresh parsley
1/2 clove of garlic, minced

2 tablespoons melted margarine
1/2 teaspoon salt
1/8 teaspoon pepper
1/4 teaspoon basil
4 tomatoes

Preheat oven to 425 degrees. Mix first 8 ingredients in bowl. Cut each tomato into 8 wedges. Place in greased 7x11-inch casserole. Sprinkle with bread crumb mixture. Bake for 8 minutes. Yield: 4 servings.

Approx Per Serving: Cal 92; Prot 2 g; Carbo 9 g; Fiber 2 g;
    T Fat 6 g; 57% Calories from Fat; Chol <1 mg; Sod 368 mg.

Scalloped Tomatoes

1 18-ounce can whole tomatoes
1 small onion, finely chopped
1 1/2 stacks unsalted crackers,
  coarsely crumbled

10 ounces sharp Cheddar cheese,
  sliced
2 tablespoons margarine
Paprika to taste

Preheat oven to 350 degrees. Mash undrained tomatoes in bowl. Layer tomatoes, onion, crackers and cheese 1/3 at a time in 1 1/2-quart casserole. Dot with margarine; sprinkle with paprika. Bake for 20 to 25 minutes or until hot and bubbly. Yield: 8 servings.

Approx Per Serving: Cal 276; Prot 11 g; Carbo 19 g; Fiber 1 g;
    T Fat 18 g; 57% Calories from Fat; Chol 37 mg; Sod 560 mg.

Zucchini Boats

3 medium zucchini
2 tablespoons margarine
2 tablespoons chopped parsley
1 tablespoon olive oil
1 tablespoon finely chopped
  onion
1 clove of garlic, minced
1 large tomato, chopped

1/2 cup fine dry bread crumbs
2 tablespoons grated Parmesan
  cheese
1/4 teaspoon salt
Black pepper and cayenne
  pepper to taste
1/2 cup shredded mozzarella
  cheese

Cut zucchini into halves lengthwise; scoop out pulp, leaving 1/4-inch shells. Place shells in 6x10-inch microwave-safe casserole. Combine margarine, parsley, olive oil, onion and garlic in microwave-safe bowl. Microwave on High for 1 1/2 to 2 minutes or until margarine is melted. Stir in tomato, bread crumbs, Parmesan cheese, zucchini pulp and seasonings. Spoon into zucchini shells. Microwave, covered with waxed paper, on High for 5 minutes. Sprinkle with mozzarella cheese. Microwave on High for 1 minute longer or until cheese is melted. Yield: 6 servings.

Approx Per Serving: Cal 145; Prot 5 g; Carbo 11 g; Fiber 2 g;
    T Fat 9 g; 55% Calories from Fat; Chol 9 mg; Sod 267 mg.

Zucchini and Peppers

1/2 cup sliced green onions
1 cup green bell pepper strips
1 cup red bell pepper strips
1 1/2 tablespoons olive oil
2 to 3 cups thin zucchini strips

1 teaspoon basil
1 teaspoon salt
1 teaspoon pepper
2 cloves of garlic, crushed
1/2 cup sliced pitted black olives

Sauté green onions and peppers in olive oil in skillet for 5 minutes. Add zucchini. Cook for 5 minutes longer or until tender-crisp. Add seasonings, garlic and olives. Spoon into serving dish. Yield: 8 servings.

Approx Per Serving: Cal 46; Prot 1 g; Carbo 3 g; Fiber 1 g;
    T Fat 4 g; 68% Calories from Fat; Chol 0 mg; Sod 309 mg.

Create a special children's table for parties and family gatherings. Use white craft paper for a tablecloth and let them design their own place mats with markers. Use toys such as plastic buckets for serving pieces and for place-marking favors.

Vegetables with Almonds

1 9-ounce package frozen
   Italian green beans
3 cups sliced carrots, cooked
1/2 cup melted margarine
1 tablespoon lemon juice
1/2 teaspoon salt
1/4 teaspoon pepper
1/2 cup sliced almonds

Cook green beans using package directions; drain. Combine green beans and carrots in serving dish. Mix margarine, lemon juice, salt, pepper and almonds in bowl. Drizzle over vegetables. Yield: 6 servings.

Approx Per Serving: Cal 209; Prot 3 g; Carbo 8 g; Fiber 3 g;
    T Fat 19 g; 80% Calories from Fat; Chol 0 mg; Sod 375 mg.

Grilled Vegetables

3 or 4 Roma tomatoes, cut into
   quarters
1 large onion, sliced
2 small zucchini, sliced
Flowerets of 1/2 bunch broccoli
Flowerets of 1/3 head cauliflower
1 tablespoon brown sugar
Sweet basil to taste
1 teaspoon instant beef bouillon
2 tablespoons margarine

Combine tomatoes, onion, zucchini, broccoli and cauliflower in bowl; mix gently. Sprinkle with brown sugar, basil and bouillon; toss gently to mix. Spread vegetables on large sheet of heavy-duty foil. Dot with margarine. Fold up foil, sealing edges. Grill over hot coals for 12 to 15 minutes or until tender. Serve hot. Yield: 6 servings.

Approx Per Serving: Cal 91; Prot 3 g; Carbo 12 g; Fiber 4 g;
    T Fat 4 g; 38% Calories from Fat; Chol 0 mg; Sod 209 mg.

Vegetable Medley with Peanut Sauce

1 pound baby carrots, peeled
1 pound fresh green beans,
   trimmed, cut into 1-inch pieces
1/4 cup minced onion
1 tablespoon margarine
1/2 teaspoon seasoned salt
1/4 cup chopped peanuts
1 1/2 teaspoons sugar
3 tablespoons chicken broth
2 tablespoons dry bread crumbs

Steam carrots in saucepan for 5 minutes. Add green beans. Steam for 6 to 7 minutes longer or until tender-crisp. Keep warm. Sauté onion in margarine in small saucepan for 4 minutes. Stir in seasoned salt and peanuts. Cook until peanuts are toasted. Stir in sugar and chicken broth. Arrange carrots spoke-fashion on serving platter. Spoon green beans in center. Drizzle with peanut sauce. Sprinkle with bread crumbs. Yield: 6 servings.

Approx Per Serving: Cal 118; Prot 4 g; Carbo 17 g; Fiber 5 g;
    T Fat 5 g; 34% Calories from Fat; Chol <1 mg; Sod 201 mg.

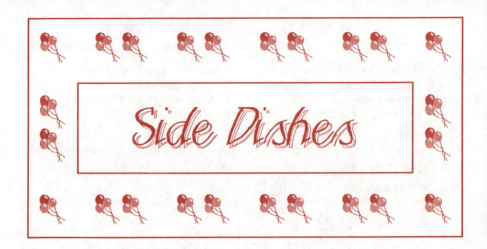

Side Dishes

Mincemeat-Glazed Apples

1 3-ounce package cherry gelatin
1 3-ounce package orange gelatin
1¹/₂ cups boiling water
1 cup cold water
8 baking apples
1¹/₂ cups prepared mincemeat

Dissolve gelatins in boiling water in bowl. Stir in cold water. Core apples and peel top ¹/₃. Arrange apples peeled end up in large skillet. Fill apple cores with mincemeat. Pour gelatin mixture over apples. Bring to a boil over medium heat; reduce heat. Simmer, covered, for 15 minutes or until apples are tender. Preheat broiler. Broil for 15 minutes or until apples are glazed and light brown, basting frequently. Serve warm or cool with ice cream. Spoon cooking syrup over top. Yield: 8 servings.

Approx Per Serving: Cal 221; Prot 3 g; Carbo 53 g; Fiber 4 g;
T Fat 2 g; 6% Calories from Fat; Chol 1 mg; Sod 105 mg.

Overnight Baked Apples

¹/₂ cup raisins
1 cup chopped pecans
1 cup packed light brown sugar
8 apples
Cinnamon and nutmeg to taste
2 tablespoons margarine
¹/₂ cup water

Mix first 3 ingredients in bowl. Peel top ¹/₃ of apples; remove core. Fill with raisin mixture. Place in slow cooker. Sprinkle with seasonings; dot with margarine. Add water. Cook on Low for 8 hours to overnight. Yield: 8 servings.

Approx Per Serving: Cal 364; Prot 2 g; Carbo 65 g; Fiber 5 g;
T Fat 13 g; 31% Calories from Fat; Chol 0 mg; Sod 51 mg.

Fresh Cranberry Relish

1 orange, cut into quarters,
   seeded
1 8-ounce can juice-pack
   crushed pineapple, drained

1 cup chopped unpeeled apple
1/3 cup sugar
2 cups fresh cranberries

Process unpeeled orange in food processor until coarsely ground. Combine with drained pineapple, apple and sugar in medium bowl; mix well. Process cranberries in food processor until coarsely ground. Add to orange mixture; mix well. Chill, covered, for 8 hours. Yield: 12 servings.

Approx Per Serving: Cal 52; Prot <1 g; Carbo 14 g; Fiber 1 g;
     T Fat <1 g; 2% Calories from Fat; Chol 0 mg; Sod 1 mg.

Baked Fruit Compote

1 8-ounce package mixed dried
   fruit
1 20-ounce can pineapple
   chunks

1 29-ounce can sliced peaches
1 20-ounce can light cherry pie
   filling

Preheat oven to 350 degrees. Chop dried fruit. Combine with pineapple, peaches and pie filling in large baking dish; mix well. Bake for 1 hour, stirring occasionally. Yield: 8 servings.

Approx Per Serving: Cal 268; Prot 2 g; Carbo 71 g; Fiber 4 g;
     T Fat <1 g; 1% Calories from Fat; Chol 0 mg; Sod 34 mg.

Zesty Orange Grits

1 cup uncooked quick-cooking
   grits
1 teaspoon salt
3 cups boiling water
1/4 cup margarine

1 teaspoon grated orange rind
1 cup orange juice
4 eggs, beaten
2 tablespoons brown sugar

Preheat oven to 350 degrees. Stir grits into salted boiling water in saucepan. Cook over medium heat for 3 minutes, stirring constantly; remove from heat. Add margarine, orange rind, orange juice and eggs; mix well. Spoon into greased 1 1/2-quart baking dish. Sprinkle with brown sugar. Bake for 45 minutes or until knife inserted in center comes out clean. Yield: 12 servings.

Approx Per Serving: Cal 126; Prot 3 g; Carbo 15 g; Fiber 2 g;
     T Fat 6 g; 42% Calories from Fat; Chol 71 mg; Sod 247 mg.

Tomato-Basil Fettucini

1/4 cup chopped onion
1 clove of garlic, minced
1/4 cup olive oil
1   28-ounce can peeled
    tomatoes, chopped
6 fresh basil leaves, chopped
1/2 teaspoon pepper

12 ounces fettucini, cooked,
    drained
1/4 cup freshly grated Parmesan
    cheese
Chopped fresh basil and chives
    to taste

Sauté onion and garlic in olive oil in skillet. Add undrained tomatoes, 6 basil leaves and pepper. Simmer, covered, for 20 minutes. Combine with fettucini in bowl; toss to mix well. Top with Parmesan cheese and additional fresh basil and chives. Yield: 6 servings.

Approx Per Serving: Cal 333; Prot 10 g; Carbo 49 g; Fiber 4 g;
    T Fat 11 g; 30% Calories from Fat; Chol 3 mg; Sod 279 mg.

Angel Hair Pasta with Dried Tomatoes

1/2 cup chopped red onion
1/3 cup chopped oil-pack
    sun-dried tomatoes
4 cloves of garlic, minced
6 fresh basil leaves, minced

2 tablespoons margarine
1   16-ounce package angel hair
    pasta, cooked, drained
1/4 cup grated Parmesan cheese

Sauté onion, tomatoes, garlic and basil in margarine in skillet for 5 to 7 minutes or until onion is transparent. Toss with pasta in bowl. Sprinkle with freshly grated Parmesan cheese. Yield: 6 servings.

Approx Per Serving: Cal 352; Prot 11 g; Carbo 59 g; Fiber <1 g;
    T Fat 7 g; 19% Calories from Fat; Chol 3 mg; Sod 109 mg.

Pasta Primavera

1   16-ounce package angel hair
    pasta
1/2 cup fresh peas
1/2 cup tiny green beans
1/2 cup sliced mushrooms

1/2 cup fresh asparagus
1/4 cup unsalted margarine
1 cup evaporated skim milk
Freshly ground pepper to taste
1/4 cup grated Parmesan cheese

Cook pasta using package directions; drain. Sauté peas, beans, mushrooms and asparagus in margarine in saucepan until tender-crisp. Add evaporated milk and pepper. Simmer until sauce is slightly thickened. Toss pasta with sauce to coat. Sprinkle with grated Parmesan cheese. Yield: 6 servings.

Approx Per Serving: Cal 415; Prot 15 g; Carbo 65 g; Fiber 1 g;
    T Fat 10 g; 22% Calories from Fat; Chol 4 mg; Sod 113 mg.

Pasta Primavera Pronto

1 16-ounce package spaghetti
2 tablespoons margarine
3/4 cup water

1 16-ounce package California-
    blend mixed vegetables
1/4 cup grated Parmesan cheese

Cook spaghetti using package directions; drain. Place in covered dish; dot with 1 tablespoon margarine. Combine remaining 1 tablespoon margarine with water and mixed vegetables in covered microwave-safe dish. Microwave on High for 3 to 5 minutes or until tender-crisp. Add to spaghetti; toss well. Sprinkle with Parmesan cheese before serving. Yield: 6 servings.

Approx Per Serving: Cal 373; Prot 13 g; Carbo 67 g; Fiber 6 g;
    T Fat 6 g; 14% Calories from Fat; Chol 3 mg; Sod 136 mg.

Tortellini and Spinach

3 9-ounce packages frozen
    creamed spinach, prepared
1/2 cup low-fat milk
2 9-ounce packages tortellini,
    cooked

1 cup chopped tomato
1/2 teaspoon dried basil
1/2 cup grated Parmesan cheese

Preheat oven to 350 degrees. Mix creamed spinach with milk in bowl. Spoon half the creamed spinach mixture into shallow 2 1/2-quart casserole. Top with half the tortellini and chopped tomato. Repeat layers with remaining creamed spinach, tortellini and tomato. Sprinkle with basil and Parmesan cheese. Bake, covered with foil, for 40 minutes. Yield: 6 servings.

Approx Per Serving: Cal 500; Prot 21 g; Carbo 51 g; Fiber <1 g;
    T Fat 24 g; 42% Calories from Fat; Chol 48 mg; Sod 1304 mg.

Pasta with Fresh Vegetables

1 clove of garlic, minced
1 1/2 cups whole kernel corn
8 ounces fresh green beans, cut
    into thirds
3 tablespoons olive oil
1/2 teaspoon each oregano and
    rosemary

1 tablespoon basil
3 tomatoes, chopped
1/4 cup chopped parsley
Juice of 1 lemon
1 16-ounce package pasta,
    cooked, drained
Salt and pepper to taste

Cook garlic, corn and beans in olive oil over medium heat in skillet until tender-crisp. Add next 6 ingredients. Simmer until heated through. Toss with pasta in bowl. Season with salt and pepper. Yield: 4 servings.

Approx Per Serving: Cal 598; Prot 18 g; Carbo 106 g; Fiber 10 g;
    T Fat 13 g; 18% Calories from Fat; Chol 0 mg; Sod 23 mg.

Pasta with White Sauce

1 16-ounce package thin
    spaghetti
2 tablespoons margarine
1 teaspoon chopped parsley

2 tablespoons olive oil
Garlic powder, salt and pepper
    to taste
Grated Parmesan cheese to taste

Cook pasta using package directions; drain but do not rinse. Combine margarine, parsley, olive oil, garlic powder, salt and pepper in bowl; toss to mix well. Top with cheese. Yield: 6 servings.

Approx Per Serving: Cal 353; Prot 10 g; Carbo 57 g; Fiber 3 g;
    T Fat 9 g; 24% Calories from Fat; Chol 0 mg; Sod 46 mg.

Apricot and Brown Rice Pilaf

1 cup shredded carrot
1 tablespoon pine nuts
1 tablespoon margarine
4 ounces quick-cooking brown
    rice

1 cup apple juice
3/4 cup water
6 dried apricot halves, chopped
2 tablespoons raisins

Combine carrot, pine nuts and margarine in 1-quart glass casserole. Microwave on High for 2 minutes. Add rice, apple juice and water. Microwave, loosely covered, for 5 minutes, stirring once. Mix in apricots and raisins. Microwave, covered, on Medium for 12 to 15 minutes or until liquid is absorbed and rice is tender. Yield: 6 servings.

Approx Per Serving: Cal 139; Prot 2 g; Carbo 27 g; Fiber 2 g;
    T Fat 3 g; 20% Calories from Fat; Chol 0 mg; Sod 33 mg.

Green Rice

3 cups cooked rice
1 cup chopped spinach
1 cup chopped parsley
2 eggs, beaten
1 cup skim milk

1/4 cup oil
1 onion, grated
3/4 cup shredded low-fat
    mozzarella cheese

Preheat oven to 350 degrees. Combine rice, spinach, parsley, eggs, milk, oil and onion in large bowl; mix well. Spoon into 9x9-inch baking dish sprayed with nonstick cooking spray. Sprinkle with cheese. Bake for 30 minutes. Cut into squares. Serve plain, with low-calorie white sauce or low-sodium mushroom sauce. Yield: 12 servings.

Approx Per Serving: Cal 141; Prot 5 g; Carbo 15 g; Fiber 1 g;
    T Fat 7 g; 43% Calories from Fat; Chol 40 mg; Sod 61 mg.

Herbed Rice

1 1/2 cups chopped onion
2 cups chopped celery
2 cups uncooked rice
1/2 cup margarine
5 cups water

2 envelopes low-sodium chicken
    noodle soup mix
2 teaspoons salt
1/2 teaspoon each thyme, sage
    and pepper

Sauté onion, celery and rice in margarine in saucepan until rice is golden brown. Stir in water, soup mix, salt, thyme, sage and pepper. Simmer, covered, for 15 minutes or until rice is tender and liquid is absorbed. Yield: 12 servings.

Approx Per Serving: Cal 230; Prot 5 g; Carbo 33 g; Fiber 1 g;
    T Fat 9 g; 34% Calories from Fat; Chol 2 mg; Sod 1455 mg.

Rice Olé

1 cup instant rice
2/3 cup water
1 cup picante sauce
1 16-ounce can Mexicorn

1 cup shredded Cheddar cheese
1 cup shredded Monterey Jack
    cheese
1/2 cup light sour cream

Preheat oven to 350 degrees. Combine rice, water, picante sauce, corn, cheeses and sour cream in 2-quart baking dish. Bake for 30 minutes. Yield: 8 servings.

Approx Per Serving: Cal 232; Prot 10 g; Carbo 23 g; Fiber 1 g;
    T Fat 11 g; 43% Calories from Fat; Chol 34 mg; Sod 512 mg.

Vegetarian Fried Rice

4 radishes, sliced
3 cups cooked brown rice
1 teaspoon rice wine vinegar
3 cloves of garlic, minced
1 teaspoon sesame oil
4 scallions, chopped

4 ounces mushrooms, thinly
    sliced
3 ounces frozen peas, thawed
2 ounces water chestnuts, sliced
1 tablespoon reduced-sodium
    soy sauce

Combine radishes, rice and vinegar in small bowl; set aside. Sauté garlic in oil in 2-quart saucepan until light brown. Add scallions and mushrooms. Sauté until tender. Add rice mixture, peas, water chestnuts and soy sauce; mix well. Simmer until heated through. Serve hot. Yield: 10 servings.

Approx Per Serving: Cal 89; Prot 2 g; Carbo 18 g; Fiber 2 g;
    T Fat 1 g; 9% Calories from Fat; Chol 0 mg; Sod 50 mg.

Veggie-Rice Sauté

1 cup instant rice
1/2 cup chopped green, red or
    yellow bell pepper
1/2 cup chopped yellow squash
1/2 cup chopped zucchini
1/4 cup chopped carrot

1 tablespoon canola oil
2 eggs
1 to 2 teaspoons reduced-sodium
    soy sauce
1/2 teaspoon poultry seasoning
Salt and pepper to taste

Cook rice using package directions. Sauté vegetables in oil in large skillet until tender. Stir in rice. Beat eggs with soy sauce and seasonings in bowl. Pour into rice mixture. Cook over medium heat, stirring constantly until eggs are firm. Yield: 6 servings.

Approx Per Serving: Cal 114; Prot 4 g; Carbo 15 g; Fiber 1 g;
    T Fat 4 g; 34% Calories from Fat; Chol 71 mg; Sod 68 mg.

Wild Rice and Mushroom Casserole

3 .6-ounce packages long grain
    and wild rice mix
4 stalks celery, chopped
4 green onions, chopped

1 green bell pepper, chopped
12 fresh mushrooms, sliced
3/4 cup evaporated skim milk

Preheat oven to 350 degrees. Cook rice using package directions. Combine rice with celery, green onions, green pepper and mushrooms in bowl; mix well. Spoon into 2-quart baking dish. Pour evaporated milk over top. Bake for 30 minutes or until bubbly, stirring several times. Yield: 12 servings.

Approx Per Serving: Cal 200; Prot 6 g; Carbo 35 g; Fiber 1 g;
    T Fat 4 g; 19% Calories from Fat; Chol 1 mg; Sod 936 mg.

San Francisco Stuffing

6 cups sourdough bread cubes
11/2 cups chopped dried apricots
1 cup chopped celery
1 cup coarsely chopped pine
    nuts or pecans

11/3 cups chopped green onions
1 cup chicken broth
1/4 cup olive oil
1 tablespoon fresh basil
1 clove of garlic, minced

Preheat oven to 375 degrees. Combine bread cubes, apricots, celery, pine nuts and green onions in large bowl; mix gently. Combine chicken broth, olive oil, basil and garlic in small bowl; mix well. Sprinkle chicken broth mixture over bread cube mixture; toss lightly to mix well. Spoon into baking dish. Bake for 40 minutes. Yield: 8 servings.

Approx Per Serving: Cal 332; Prot 6 g; Carbo 46 g; Fiber 6 g;
    T Fat 17 g; 43% Calories from Fat; Chol <1 mg; Sod 241 mg.

Monterey Strata

4 cups cheese-flavored tortilla
    chips
2 cups shredded Monterey Jack
    cheese
6 eggs, beaten
2¹/₂ cups low-fat milk

1 4-ounce can chopped green
    chilies
1 cup chopped onion
3 tablespoons catsup
¹/₄ teaspoon Tabasco sauce
¹/₂ teaspoon salt

Layer tortilla chips and cheese in greased 9x13-inch baking dish. Combine remaining ingredients in bowl; mix well. Pour over layers. Chill overnight. Preheat oven to 325 degrees. Bake casserole for 50 minutes or until set. Yield: 8 servings.

Approx Per Serving: Cal 307; Prot 16 g; Carbo 19 g; Fiber 1 g;
    T Fat 19 g; 55% Calories from Fat; Chol 193 mg; Sod 631 mg.

Scrambled Egg Casserole

2¹/₂ tablespoons all-purpose flour
2 tablespoons melted margarine
2 cups low-fat milk
¹/₂ teaspoon salt
¹/₄ teaspoon pepper
8 ounces light cream cheese,
    cubed
¹/₄ cup chopped green onions
3 tablespoons melted margarine

12 eggs, beaten
¹/₂ teaspoon salt
¹/₂ teaspoon pepper
1 4-ounce can sliced
    mushrooms, drained
2¹/₄ cups bread crumbs
¹/₂ cup melted margarine
¹/₄ teaspoon paprika

Blend flour into 2 tablespoons margarine in heavy saucepan. Cook for 1 minute. Add milk gradually. Cook over medium heat until thickened, stirring constantly. Add ¹/₂ teaspoon salt, ¹/₄ teaspoon pepper and cream cheese; mix until smooth. Remove from heat. Sauté green onions in 3 tablespoons margarine in large skillet. Add eggs, ¹/₂ teaspoon salt and ¹/₂ teaspoon pepper. Cook until soft-set, stirring frequently. Add mushrooms and cheese sauce. Spoon into greased 9x13-inch baking dish. Toss bread crumbs with ¹/₂ cup melted margarine. Spread over casserole; sprinkle with paprika. Chill, covered, overnight. Preheat oven to 350 degrees. Bake for 30 minutes or until heated through. Yield: 12 servings.

Approx Per Serving: Cal 333; Prot 12 g; Carbo 19 g; Fiber 1 g;
    T Fat 23 g; 62% Calories from Fat; Chol 228 mg; Sod 698 mg.

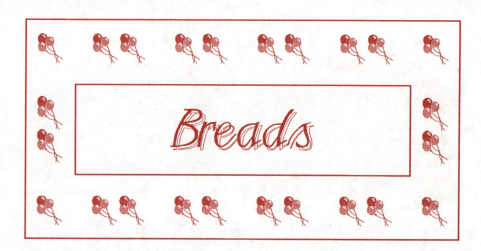

Breads

Barbecued Biscuits

¹/₄ cup milk
1 teaspoon chopped parsley
1 teaspoon Worcestershire sauce
¹/₄ cup chili sauce

¹/₂ teaspoon instant minced
  onion
2 cups baking mix

Preheat oven to 450 degrees. Combine milk, parsley, Worcestershire sauce, chili sauce and minced onion in bowl; mix well. Let stand for 5 minutes. Stir in baking mix. Shape into ball on floured surface. Knead 5 times. Roll out to ¹/₂-inch thickness. Cut into 2-inch rounds; place on ungreased baking sheet. Reroll remaining dough; cut into rounds. Bake for 8 to 10 minutes or until brown. Yield: 10 servings.

Approx Per Serving: Cal 120; Prot 2 g; Carbo 19 g; Fiber <1 g;
    T Fat 4 g; 29% Calories from Fat; Chol 1 mg; Sod 416 mg.

Cheese-Garlic Biscuits

2 cups baking mix
²/₃ cup milk
¹/₂ cup shredded Cheddar cheese

¹/₄ cup melted margarine
¹/₄ teaspoon garlic powder

Preheat oven to 450 degrees. Combine baking mix, milk and cheese in bowl; mix well. Add margarine and garlic powder. Beat for 30 seconds. Drop by spoonfuls onto ungreased baking sheet. Bake for 8 to 10 minutes or until brown. Yield: 10 servings.

Approx Per Serving: Cal 182; Prot 4 g; Carbo 18 g; Fiber 0 g;
    T Fat 11 g; 53% Calories from Fat; Chol 8 mg; Sod 413 mg.

Parmesan Biscuits

2 tablespoons margarine
2 tablespoons grated Parmesan
  cheese

1   10-count can biscuits

Preheat oven to 400 degrees. Melt margarine in baking pan in oven. Sprinkle cheese over margarine. Separate biscuits. Place in pan, turning to coat both sides. Bake for 8 to 9 minutes or until brown. Yield: 10 servings.

Approx Per Serving: Cal 90; Prot 2 g; Carbo 10 g; Fiber <1 g;
    T Fat 5 g; 48% Calories from Fat; Chol 2 mg; Sod 295 mg.

Holiday Scones

4 cups all-purpose flour
3 tablespoons sugar
1 tablespoon baking powder
$1/2$ teaspoon baking soda
$1/2$ teaspoon salt
$2/3$ cup margarine

$1^1/3$ cups buttermilk
8 teaspoons cherry jam or
  preserves
1 tablespoon sugar
2 tablespoons red sugar sprinkles

Preheat oven to 425 degrees. Combine first 5 ingredients in bowl. Cut in margarine until crumbly. Add buttermilk; mix lightly with fork until mixture forms soft dough. Knead dough gently 5 or 6 times on lightly floured surface. Roll $1/4$ inch thick; cut into sixteen 3-inch circles. Place 8 circles on greased baking sheet. Spoon 1 teaspoon cherry jam into center of each. Moisten edges with water; top with remaining circles, pressing edges to seal. Sprinkle with mixture of 1 tablespoon sugar and red sugar sprinkles. Bake for 15 minutes or until golden brown. Serve warm. Yield: 8 servings.

Approx Per Serving: Cal 436; Prot 8 g; Carbo 64 g; Fiber 2 g;
    T Fat 16 g; 34% Calories from Fat; Chol 2 mg; Sod 531 mg.

Rosemary-Topped Breadsticks

1   10-count can soft breadsticks
1 egg white, lightly beaten
Salt to taste

1 to $1^1/2$ teaspoons dried
  rosemary
1 to $1^1/2$ teaspoons dried chives

Preheat oven to 350 degrees. Unroll dough; separate at perforations into 10 breadsticks. Twist each breadstick; place on ungreased baking sheet, pressing down ends to keep bread twisted. Brush tops of breadsticks with egg white; salt lightly. Sprinkle rosemary and chives on top. Bake for 15 to 18 minutes or until brown. Yield: 10 servings.

Approx Per Serving: Cal 102; Prot 3 g; Carbo 17 g; Fiber 0 g;
    T Fat 2 g; 18% Calories from Fat; Chol 0 mg; Sod 235 mg.

Cheesy Breadsticks

1 1/2 cups all-purpose flour
2 teaspoons baking powder
1 teaspoon sugar
1 teaspoon salt
1/2 cup shredded Cheddar cheese
2/3 cup milk

2 tablespoons margarine,
  softened
1 egg, beaten
Onion salt, garlic salt or herbs to
  taste

Preheat oven to 400 degrees. Mix flour, baking powder, sugar and salt in bowl. Stir in cheese. Add milk and margarine; mix with fork to form soft dough. Knead 10 times on lightly floured surface. Roll into 12x16-inch rectangle. Cut into 3/4x8-inch strips. Place on greased baking sheet. Brush with beaten egg; sprinkle with onion salt, garlic salt or herbs to taste. Bake for 15 to 20 minutes or until golden brown. Remove to wire rack to cool. Yield: 10 servings.

Approx Per Serving: Cal 132; Prot 5 g; Carbo 16 g; Fiber 1 g;
    T Fat 5 g; 38% Calories from Fat; Chol 30 mg; Sod 355 mg.

Zesty Breadsticks

1   8-count can crescent rolls
2 eggs
2 tablespoons melted margarine
1 teaspoon all-purpose flour
1/4 teaspoon onion salt

1/2 teaspoon garlic powder
1/2 teaspoon parsley flakes
2   3-ounce cans French-fried
    onions, crushed

Preheat oven to 375 degrees. Unroll crescent roll dough. Cut into 32 strips. Combine eggs, margarine, flour, onion salt, garlic powder and parsley flakes in bowl; mix well. Dip each dough strip in mixture to coat; roll in crushed onions. Place on baking sheet. Bake for 10 minutes. May twist each strip before baking. Yield: 10 servings.

Approx Per Serving: Cal 222; Prot 4 g; Carbo 16 g; Fiber <1 g;
    T Fat 16 g; 64% Calories from Fat; Chol 43 mg; Sod 376 mg.

Fill an hors d'oeuvres basket with fresh vegetable and breadstick dippers or with fruit and cookies. Nestle bowl of dip among the goodies.

Festive Blueberry Pizza Coffee Cake

8 ounces light cream cheese,
    softened
1/2 cup sugar
1 egg, beaten
1 teaspoon vanilla extract
1 loaf frozen bread dough,
    thawed
2 cups blueberries

3/4 cup all-purpose flour
1/2 cup sugar
6 tablespoons margarine
1/4 teaspoon butter extract
1 cup confectioners' sugar
2 tablespoons milk
1/2 teaspoon vanilla extract

Beat cream cheese with 1/2 cup sugar in small mixer bowl until light and fluffy. Beat in egg and 1 teaspoon vanilla. Press thawed bread dough into 14-inch pizza pan. Spread with cream cheese mixture. Sprinkle with blueberries. Mix flour and 1/2 cup sugar in small bowl. Cut in margarine and butter extract until crumbly. Spoon over blueberries. Let rise for 30 minutes. Preheat oven to 375 degrees. Bake coffee cake for 30 minutes or until golden brown. Blend confectioners' sugar with milk and 1/2 teaspoon vanilla in bowl. Drizzle over warm coffee cake. Yield: 10 servings.

Approx Per Serving: Cal 408; Prot 8 g; Carbo 69 g; Fiber 1 g;
    T Fat 13 g; 28% Calories from Fat; Chol 35 mg; Sod 496 mg.

Cranberry and Yogurt Coffee Cake

1 2-layer package yellow cake
   mix
1 4-ounce package vanilla
   instant pudding mix
4 eggs

1 cup plain nonfat yogurt
1/4 cup oil
1 16-ounce can whole cranberry
   sauce
1/2 cup chopped walnuts

Preheat oven to 350 degrees. Mix dry cake mix and pudding mix in large mixer bowl. Add eggs, yogurt and oil. Beat at high speed for 3 minutes. Pour 2/3 of the batter into greased 9x13-inch baking pan. Spoon cranberry sauce over batter. Top with remaining batter. Sprinkle with walnuts. Bake for 45 to 50 minutes or until coffee cake tests done. Yield: 12 servings.

Approx Per Serving: Cal 384; Prot 6 g; Carbo 62 g; Fiber 1 g;
    T Fat 13 g; 30% Calories from Fat; Chol 71 mg; Sod 374 mg.

Peach Coffee Cake

2 tablespoons light brown sugar
2 tablespoons all-purpose flour
2 tablespoons oats
1/2 teaspoon cinnamon
2 tablespoons margarine
1 pound frozen bread dough,
    thawed

1   21-ounce can peach pie filling
2 tablespoons melted margarine
1 cup confectioners' sugar
1 teaspoon vanilla extract
1 tablespoon milk

Mix brown sugar, flour, oats and cinnamon in bowl. Cut in 2 tablespoons margarine until crumbly. Roll bread dough into 8x12-inch rectangle on lightly floured surface. Place dough on greased baking sheet. Cut 2-inch strips at 1-inch intervals toward center with kitchen shears along the 12-inch sides. Spoon peach pie filling lengthwise down center of dough. Fold strips alternately across pie filling for a braided look. Brush top with melted margarine; sprinkle with brown sugar mixture. Let rise in warm area until puffy. Bake in preheated 350-degree oven for 30 to 35 minutes or until golden brown. Cool. Combine confectioners' sugar, vanilla and milk in bowl; mix well. Drizzle over coffee cake. Yield: 10 servings.

Approx Per Serving: Cal 278; Prot 4 g; Carbo 56 g; Fiber 1 g;
    T Fat 6 g; 19% Calories from Fat; Chol <1 mg; Sod 349 mg.

Healthy Almond-Poppy Seed Loaf

1 1/2 cups all-purpose flour
2 teaspoons baking powder
1/4 teaspoon salt
2 teaspoons poppy seed
1 cup milk
2 eggs

1/3 cup oil
1 cup crushed All-Bran cereal
1 teaspoon vanilla extract
1/4 teaspoon almond extract
1/2 cup toasted chopped almonds

Preheat oven to 350 degrees. Mix flour, baking powder, salt and poppy seed in bowl. Combine milk, eggs, oil, cereal, vanilla and almond extract in large mixer bowl; beat until smooth. Let stand for 2 minutes or until cereal is softened. Stir in almonds. Add mixture of dry ingredients; mix just until moistened. Spread in greased and floured 5x9-inch loaf pan. Bake for 45 minutes or until bread tests done. Cool in pan for 10 minutes. Remove to wire rack to cool completely. Yield: 12 servings.

Approx Per Serving: Cal 189; Prot 6 g; Carbo 20 g; Fiber 3 g;
    T Fat 11 g; 50% Calories from Fat; Chol 38 mg; Sod 201 mg.

Apricot Whole Wheat Loaf

1/2 cup packed light brown sugar
2 cups whole wheat flour
2 teaspoons baking soda
1/4 teaspoon cinnamon
1/2 cup egg substitute

2   16-ounce cans juice-pack
     apricots, drained, puréed
1/4 cup safflower oil
2 teaspoons vanilla extract

Preheat oven to 350 degrees. Combine brown sugar, whole wheat flour, baking soda and cinnamon in bowl. Mix egg substitute, apricot purée, oil and vanilla in bowl. Add to dry ingredients, mixing until just blended; do not over mix. Pour into greased and floured 5x9-inch loaf pan. Bake for 55 minutes or until loaf tests done. Cool in pan for several minutes. Remove to wire rack to cool completely. Yield: 12 servings.

Approx Per Serving: Cal 195; Prot 4 g; Carbo 35 g; Fiber 4 g;
     T Fat 5 g; 23% Calories from Fat; Chol <1 mg; Sod 164 mg.

Avocado-Pecan Bread

1 egg
1/2 cup buttermilk
1/3 cup oil
2 tablespoons margarine,
    softened
1/2 cup mashed avocado

2 cups all-purpose flour
3/4 cup sugar
1/2 teaspoon baking soda
1/2 teaspoon baking powder
1/4 teaspoon salt
3/4 cup chopped pecans

Preheat oven to 350 degrees. Combine egg, buttermilk, oil, margarine and avocado in mixer bowl; beat well. Add flour, sugar, baking soda, baking powder and salt; mix well. Stir in pecans. Pour into 3 greased 3x5-inch loaf pans. Bake for 30 minutes or until loaves test done. Cool in pans for 10 minutes. Remove to serving plate. Serve warm with cream cheese, butter or margarine. Yield: 12 servings.

Approx Per Serving: Cal 270; Prot 4 g; Carbo 31 g; Fiber 2 g;
     T Fat 15 g; 50% Calories from Fat; Chol 18 mg; Sod 133 mg.

Keep a journal of special occasions and include the guest list, menu, recipes and decorations.

Banapple Bread

2 eggs
2 very ripe bananas, mashed
1 teaspoon vanilla extract
1 teaspoon cinnamon
1 teaspoon allspice
¹⁄₄ cup honey
2 cups flour

2 teaspoons baking powder
1 teaspoon baking soda
¹⁄₂ teaspoon salt
¹⁄₃ cup raisins
2 Granny Smith apples, peeled,
   chopped

Preheat oven to 375 degrees. Combine eggs, bananas, vanilla, spices and honey in mixer bowl. Beat until blended. Add mixture of dry ingredients; mix well. Fold in raisins and apples. Spoon into greased and floured 5x9-inch loaf pan. Bake for 40 to 45 minutes or until loaf tests done. Remove to wire rack to cool completely. Yield: 12 servings.

Approx Per Serving: Cal 155; Prot 4 g; Carbo 33 g; Fiber 2 g;
    T Fat 1 g; 7% Calories from Fat; Chol 36 mg; Sod 225 mg.

Cheddar-Garlic Bread

2 frozen loaves bread dough
1 teaspoon minced garlic
¹⁄₄ cup chopped green onion tops

¹⁄₂ cup shredded Cheddar cheese
3 tablespoons melted margarine

Thaw bread in refrigerator overnight. Place in greased bowl, turning to grease surface. Let dough rise in warm place. Roll dough into rectangle on floured surface. Sprinkle with garlic, onion tops and cheese. Roll to enclose filling. Turn open ends under; place in greased 5x9-inch loaf pan. Cut 3 to 5 slashes in top. Let rise in warm place for 1 hour. Drizzle with margarine. Bake in preheated 375-degree oven for 30 to 40 minutes or until brown. Remove to wire rack to cool. Yield: 12 servings.

Approx Per Serving: Cal 234; Prot 7 g; Carbo 41 g; Fiber <1 g;
    T Fat 7 g; 25% Calories from Fat; Chol 5 mg; Sod 522 mg.

Use your slow cooker as a bread warmer for a party. Place a damp cloth inside the slow cooker and heat on Low for 30 minutes. Remove cloth and line with large napkins. Place bread inside. Bread will remain hot for up to 2 hours.

Bubble Loaves

1/4 cup melted margarine
1/2 teaspoon garlic powder
1 egg, beaten
1/4 teaspoon salt

1 teaspoon dried parsley flakes
1 16-ounce package frozen roll
   dough, thawed
2 tablespoons melted margarine

Combine 1/4 cup margarine, garlic powder, egg, salt and parsley flakes in bowl; mix well. Dip rolls in seasoned margarine; place in 3 greased 3x5-inch loaf pans. Let rise, covered, in warm place until doubled in bulk. Bake in preheated 350-degree oven for 30 minutes. Brush with melted margarine. Remove to wire racks to cool. Yield: 12 servings.

Approx Per Serving: Cal 152; Prot 3 g; Carbo 20 g; Fiber 0 g;
    T Fat 8 g; 42% Calories from Fat; Chol 18 mg; Sod 347 mg.

Cheesy Ham and Broccoli Bread

2 loaves frozen honey wheat
   bread dough, thawed
1 cup shredded ham

1 cup shredded Cheddar cheese
1 cup chopped broccoli,
   blanched, drained

Flatten bread dough on greased baking pan. Sprinkle with ham, cheese and broccoli. Roll to enclose filling. Place in 5x9-inch loaf pan. Let rise until doubled in bulk. Bake using bread dough package directions. Slice and serve hot with coarse mustard. Yield: 12 servings.

Approx Per Serving: Cal 261; Prot 12 g; Carbo 40 g; Fiber <1 g;
    T Fat 6 g; 21% Calories from Fat; Chol 16 mg; Sod 215 mg.

Easy Herb Bread

3 tablespoons margarine
1 tablespoon dried minced onion
2 teaspoons dillseed
1 teaspoon sesame seed

1/4 teaspoon celery seed
1 10-count can biscuits
1/4 cup grated Parmesan cheese

Preheat oven to 400 degrees. Met margarine in 8-inch baking pan. Sprinkle onion, dillseed, sesame seed and celery seed over melted margarine. Separate biscuits; cut into quarters. Coat with Parmesan cheese; arrange in baking pan. Sprinkle with remaining Parmesan cheese. Bake for 15 to 18 minutes or until golden brown. Invert onto serving plate. Yield: 6 servings.

Approx Per Serving: Cal 180; Prot 4 g; Carbo 17 g; Fiber 1 g;
    T Fat 11 g; 53% Calories from Fat; Chol 4 mg; Sod 545 mg.

Lemon Yogurt Bread

3 cups all-purpose flour
1 teaspoon each salt, baking
  soda and baking powder
1³/₄ cups sugar
3 eggs

1 cup oil
2 tablespoons lemon extract
1 tablespoon grated lemon rind
2 cups lemon yogurt
1 cup chopped almonds

Preheat oven to 325 degrees. Combine first 5 ingredients in mixer bowl. Add eggs, oil, lemon extract, lemon rind and yogurt; beat until well mixed. Stir in almonds. Pour into 2 greased 5x9-inch loaf pans. Bake for 45 to 60 minutes or until loaves test done. Cool in pans for 10 minutes. Remove to wire rack to cool completely. Yield: 24 servings.

Approx Per Serving: Cal 255; Prot 4 g; Carbo 31 g; Fiber 1 g;
    T Fat 13 g; 46% Calories from Fat; Chol 28 mg; Sod 159 mg.

Olive Bread

¹/₂ cup margarine, softened
1   4-ounce can chopped black
    olives, drained
4 green onions, chopped

1 cup shredded Velveeta cheese
1 teaspoon garlic salt
2 loaves French bread, split

Preheat oven to 350 degrees. Mix first 5 ingredients in bowl. Spread mixture on bottom halves of bread; replace tops. Slice bread to, but not through bottom. Wrap in foil. Bake for 20 to 25 minutes. Yield: 20 servings.

Approx Per Serving: Cal 202; Prot 6 g; Carbo 23 g; Fiber 1 g;
    T Fat 9 g; 42% Calories from Fat; Chol 5 mg; Sod 543 mg.

Orange-Date-Nut Bread

1   2-layer package orange
    supreme cake mix
1   12-ounce can date spread
1   5-ounce can evaporated milk
2 eggs, beaten

¹/₂ cup chopped pecans
³/₄ cup chopped orange sections
¹/₂ cup confectioners' sugar
1 tablespoon water
¹/₄ teaspoon orange extract

Preheat oven to 350 degrees. Combine cake mix, date spread, evaporated milk and eggs in mixer bowl. Beat for 2 minutes. Stir in pecans and chopped orange sections. Pour into greased and floured 10-cup bundt pan. Bake for 40 to 50 minutes or until bread tests done. Cool in pan on wire rack for 10 minutes. Invert onto wire rack. Blend confectioners' sugar, water and orange extract in small bowl. Drizzle over bread. Yield: 12 servings.

Approx Per Serving: Cal 401; Prot 8 g; Carbo 58 g; Fiber 6 g;
    T Fat 16 g; 36% Calories from Fat; Chol 39 mg; Sod 289 mg.

Spicy Picante Bread

2 cups all-purpose flour
³/₄ cup sugar
1 teaspoon baking soda
1 teaspoon baking powder
¹/₂ teaspoon cumin

¹/₂ teaspoon cinnamon
¹/₂ teaspoon allspice
1¹/₂ cups picante sauce
¹/₂ cup melted margarine
2 eggs, beaten

Preheat oven to 350 degrees. Combine flour, sugar, baking soda, baking powder, cumin, cinnamon and allspice in mixer bowl; mix well. Add picante sauce, margarine and eggs; beat well. Spoon into 3 greased and floured 3x5-inch loaf pans. Bake for 25 minutes or until loaves test done. Remove to wire racks to cool. Yield: 12 servings.

Approx Per Serving: Cal 219; Prot 4 g; Carbo 31 g; Fiber 1 g;
T Fat 9 g; 37% Calories from Fat; Chol 36 mg; Sod 357 mg.

Marbled Pumpkin Bread

8 ounces light cream cheese,
  softened
¹/₄ cup sugar
1 egg, beaten
1³/₄ cups all-purpose flour
1¹/₂ cups sugar
1 teaspoon baking soda

1 teaspoon cinnamon
¹/₂ teaspoon salt
¹/₄ teaspoon nutmeg
1 cup canned pumpkin
¹/₂ cup melted margarine
1 egg, beaten
¹/₃ cup water

Preheat oven to 350 degrees. Blend cream cheese with ¹/₄ cup sugar and 1 egg in small bowl; set aside. Mix flour, 1¹/₂ cups sugar, baking soda, cinnamon, salt and nutmeg in large bowl. Add pumpkin, margarine, 1 egg and water; mix just until moistened. Reserve 2 cups pumpkin batter. Pour remaining pumpkin batter into greased and floured 5x9-inch loaf pan. Add cream cheese mixture and reserved pumpkin batter. Cut through with knife to marbleize. Bake for 1 hour and 10 minutes or until loaf tests done. Cool in pan for 10 minutes. Remove to wire rack to cool completely.
Yield: 12 servings.

Approx Per Serving: Cal 309; Prot 5 g; Carbo 46 g; Fiber 1 g;
T Fat 12 g; 34% Calories from Fat; Chol 46 mg; Sod 368 mg.

Add chopped celery and onion to your favorite corn bread recipe and bake it in advance. It will be ready for your holiday corn bread dressing with the addition of eggs, turkey broth and seasonings. Add pecans for a special treat.

Chocolate Zucchini Bread

1½ cups all-purpose flour
¼ teaspoon baking powder
½ teaspoon salt
½ teaspoon baking soda
2 eggs
1 cup sugar
½ cup oil

1 teaspoon vanilla extract
1 ounce unsweetened baking
  chocolate, melted
1 tablespoon melted margarine
1 cup shredded zucchini
½ cup chopped walnuts

Preheat oven to 350 degrees. Sift flour, baking powder, salt and baking soda together. Set aside. Beat eggs, sugar, oil and vanilla in mixer bowl until smooth. Add sifted dry ingredients; mix well. Stir in chocolate, margarine, zucchini and walnuts. Pour into greased and floured 5x9-inch loaf pan. Bake for 40 to 45 minutes or until loaf tests done. Remove to wire rack to cool. Yield: 12 servings.

Approx Per Serving: Cal 209; Prot 4 g; Carbo 35 g; Fiber 1 g;
    T Fat 6 g; 27% Calories from Fat; Chol 36 mg; Sod 154 mg.

Baked Apple Muffins

1 cup shredded apple
½ teaspoon grated orange rind
1 cup nonfat vanilla yogurt
2 eggs, beaten
3 cups all-purpose flour
1 cup sugar

3½ teaspoons baking powder
1 teaspoon salt
¼ teaspoon nutmeg
¾ cup margarine
½ cup melted margarine
¼ cup cinnamon-sugar

Preheat oven to 350 degrees. Combine apple, orange rind, yogurt and eggs in bowl; mix well. Sift flour, 1 cup sugar, baking powder, salt and nutmeg into large bowl. Cut in ¾ cup margarine until crumbly. Add apple mixture; mix well. Fill greased muffin cups ⅔ full. Bake for 20 to 25 minutes or until golden brown. Roll hot muffins in melted margarine; coat with cinnamon-sugar. Cool on wire rack. Yield: 12 servings.

Approx Per Serving: Cal 401; Prot 6 g; Carbo 50 g; Fiber 1 g;
    T Fat 20 g; 45% Calories from Fat; Chol 36 mg; Sod 523 mg.

Almond-Orange Muffins

1¹/₄ cups all-purpose flour
2 teaspoons baking powder
¹/₄ teaspoon salt
1 cup crushed All-Bran cereal
¹/₂ cup packed light brown sugar
³/₄ cup low-fat milk

¹/₃ cup orange juice
2 teaspoons grated orange rind
1 egg
¹/₄ cup oil
¹/₂ cup toasted chopped almonds

Preheat oven to 400 degrees. Mix flour, baking powder and salt in bowl; set aside. Combine cereal, brown sugar, milk, orange juice and orange rind in large bowl; mix well. Let stand for 2 minutes or until cereal is softened. Add egg and oil; mix well. Stir in almonds. Add dry ingredients; mix just until moistened. Spoon into 12 greased 2¹/₂-inch muffin cups. Bake for 18 to 20 minutes or until light brown. Remove to wire rack to cool.
Yield: 12 servings.

Approx Per Serving: Cal 196; Prot 5 g; Carbo 29 g; Fiber 3 g;
T Fat 8 g; 35% Calories from Fat; Chol 18 mg; Sod 200 mg.

Blueberry-Lemon Muffins

1³/₄ cups all-purpose flour
¹/₃ cup sugar
³/₄ teaspoon salt
2¹/₂ teaspoons baking powder
1 egg, beaten
1 cup nonfat lemon yogurt

¹/₃ cup oil
2 tablespoons milk
1 teaspoon finely grated lemon
    rind
³/₄ cup fresh or frozen
    blueberries

Preheat oven to 400 degrees. Combine flour, sugar, salt and baking powder in mixer bowl; mix well. Make a well in center of mixture. Beat egg, yogurt, oil, milk and lemon rind in small bowl. Add to well in dry ingredients; stir just until moistened. Fold in blueberries gently. Fill greased muffin cups ²/₃ full. Bake for 20 to 25 minutes or until golden brown. Serve warm.
Yield: 12 servings.

Approx Per Serving: Cal 166; Prot 4 g; Carbo 23 g; Fiber 1 g;
T Fat 7 g; 37% Calories from Fat; Chol 18 mg; Sod 224 mg.

Jelly Muffins

2 cups all-purpose flour
1 tablespoon baking powder
2 tablespoons sugar
1 teaspoon salt
2 egg whites

1/3 cup oil
11/4 cups skim milk
2 tablespoons jelly or jam
2 tablespoons sugar

Preheat oven to 425 degrees. Sift first 4 ingredients into bowl; make well in center. Add egg whites, oil and milk; mix just until moistened. Fill greased muffin cups 2/3 full. Drop 1/2 teaspoon jelly into center of each muffin. Sprinkle each with 1/2 teaspoon sugar. Bake for 22 minutes. Yield: 12 servings.

Approx Per Serving: Cal 166; Prot 4 g; Carbo 24 g; Fiber 1 g;
    T Fat 6 g; 34% Calories from Fat; Chol <1 mg; Sod 283 mg.

Lemon-Raspberry Muffins

2 cups baking mix
1 cup sugar
2 eggs
1 cup evaporated skim milk

1/2 cup oil
1 teaspoon lemon extract
1 cup raspberries

Preheat oven to 425 degrees. Combine baking mix and sugar in large bowl. Beat eggs in bowl. Add evaporated milk, oil and lemon extract; beat well. Add to dry ingredients; stir just until moistened. Fold in raspberries. Fill greased muffin cups 3/4 full. Bake for 18 minutes or until brown. Cool in pan for 5 minutes. Remove to wire rack to cool or serve hot. Yield: 12 servings.

Approx Per Serving: Cal 270; Prot 4 g; Carbo 34 g; Fiber 1 g;
    T Fat 13 g; 43% Calories from Fat; Chol 36 mg; Sod 301 mg.

Morning Glory Muffins

2 cups oat bran cereal
1/4 cup packed light brown sugar
2 teaspoons baking powder
1/2 teaspoon salt
2 eggs, beaten
1/2 cup orange juice

2 tablespoons grated orange rind
1/4 cup honey
2 medium bananas, mashed
2 tablespoons oil
1/2 cup chopped walnuts

Preheat oven to 425 degrees. Combine cereal, brown sugar, baking powder and salt in large bowl; mix well. Beat eggs with remaining ingredients in bowl. Stir into dry ingredients just until moistened. Fill nonstick muffin cups 2/3 full. Bake for 27 minutes. Yield: 12 servings.

Approx Per Serving: Cal 154; Prot 3 g; Carbo 23 g; Fiber 1 g;
    T Fat 7 g; 36% Calories from Fat; Chol 36 mg; Sod 214 mg.

Sunshine Muffins

1 2-layer package orange
   supreme cake mix
1/3 cup oil
1 cup orange juice
3 eggs

1 11-ounce can mandarin
   oranges, drained, chopped
1/2 cup orange juice
2 cups confectioners' sugar

Preheat oven to 350 degrees. Combine first 4 ingredients in mixer bowl. Beat for 3 minutes. Fold in chopped mandarin oranges. Pour into greased and floured or paper-lined miniature muffin cups. Bake for 10 minutes. Let stand for several minutes; remove muffins. Place on wire rack. Combine remaining 1/2 cup orange juice and confectioners' sugar in bowl; mix well. Spoon over muffins. Let stand to cool completely. Yield: 24 servings.

Approx Per Serving: Cal 181; Prot 2 g; Carbo 31 g; Fiber <1 g;
   T Fat 6 g; 27% Calories from Fat; Chol 27 mg; Sod 141 mg.

Pumpkin and Apple Streusel Muffins

2 1/2 cups all-purpose flour
2 cups sugar
1 tablespoon pumpkin pie spice
1 teaspoon baking soda
1/2 teaspoon salt
2 eggs, beaten
1 cup canned pumpkin

1/2 cup oil
2 cups chopped peeled apples
1 cup chopped pecans
2 tablespoons all-purpose flour
1/4 cup sugar
1/2 teaspoon cinnamon
4 teaspoons margarine

Preheat oven to 350 degrees. Mix 2 1/2 cups flour, 2 cups sugar, pumpkin pie spice, baking soda and salt in large bowl. Beat eggs with pumpkin and oil in bowl. Add to dry ingredients; mix just until moistened. Stir in apples and pecans. Fill greased muffin cups 3/4 full. Combine 2 tablespoons flour, 1/4 cup sugar and cinnamon in small bowl. Cut in margarine until crumbly. Sprinkle over muffin batter. Bake for 35 to 40 minutes or until golden brown. Yield: 18 servings.

Approx Per Serving: Cal 290; Prot 3 g; Carbo 44 g; Fiber 2 g;
   T Fat 12 g; 37% Calories from Fat; Chol 24 mg; Sod 124 mg.

For a brunch treat, butter toasted English muffins, drizzle with honey and sprinkle with almonds. Broil until heated through.

Starfruit Muffins

1/2 cup margarine, softened
1/3 cup sugar
1 tablespoon molasses
1 egg
1 cup all-purpose flour
1/2 cup whole wheat flour
1/2 cup quick-cooking oats
1/2 teaspoon baking powder
1 teaspoon baking soda

1/2 teaspoon cinnamon
1/4 teaspoon salt
1 cup buttermilk
1/4 cup chopped starfruit
1/4 cup sweetened coconut
1 tablespoon grated lemon rind
12 slices starfruit
1/2 cup confectioners' sugar

Preheat oven to 375 degrees. Cream margarine and sugar in mixer bowl until light and fluffy. Beat in molasses and egg. Mix all-purpose flour, whole wheat flour, oats, baking powder, baking soda, cinnamon and salt together. Add to creamed mixture alternately with buttermilk, beginning and ending with dry ingredients and mixing well after each addition. Fold in chopped starfruit, coconut and lemon rind. Spoon into 12 greased 2 1/2-inch muffin cups filling 2/3 full. Top each with starfruit slice. Bake for 20 to 25 minutes or until golden brown. Cool in pan for 5 minutes. Remove to wire rack to cool completely. Sprinkle with confectioners' sugar. Yield: 15 servings.

Approx Per Serving: Cal 168; Prot 3 g; Carbo 23 g; Fiber 2 g;
T Fat 7 g; 39% Calories from Fat; Chol 15 mg; Sod 196 mg.

Yogurt Muffins

1 1/2 cups flour
1 cup sugar
2 teaspoons baking powder
1/2 teaspoon salt
1/2 cup oil

2 eggs
8 ounces yogurt
1 cup coconut
1/3 cup sugar
1 teaspoon cinnamon

Preheat oven to 350 degrees. Mix flour, 1 cup sugar, baking powder and salt in bowl. Combine oil, eggs and yogurt in mixer bowl. Add to dry ingredients. Beat for 3 minutes. Fill paper-lined muffin cups half full. Mix coconut, 1/3 cup sugar and cinnamon in small bowl. Sprinkle over muffins. Bake for 20 to 25 minutes or until light brown. Yield: 20 servings.

Approx Per Serving: Cal 166; Prot 2 g; Carbo 23 g; Fiber 1 g;
T Fat 8 g; 41% Calories from Fat; Chol 23 mg; Sod 100 mg.

Grand Finales

If you think that the four main food groups are cookies, cakes, mousse and sundaes, this is the place for you. There's nothing like a special dessert to give a sweet ending to holiday menus. We've included a collection of beautiful ways to wind up your celebrations in style with light and easy recipes for all kinds of desserts, cakes, pies, cookies, candy and sweet beverages. If you're a believer that "Life is short: Eat dessert first," you may even want to start with this chapter and put together a dessert party for your celebration featuring a variety of these wonderful, mouth-watering treats.

Desserts

Zesty Apple Betty

5 cups sliced peeled apples
1/2 teaspoon cinnamon-sugar
1 teaspoon grated lemon rind
1 teaspoon grated orange rind
2 tablespoons orange juice
   concentrate

2 teaspoons almond extract
3/4 cup sugar
1/4 cup packed dark brown sugar
3/4 cup all-purpose flour
1/4 teaspoon salt
1/2 cup margarine, softened

Preheat oven to 350 degrees. Arrange apples in greased 2-quart baking dish. Sprinkle with cinnamon-sugar, lemon rind, orange rind, orange juice concentrate and almond extract. Combine sugar, brown sugar, flour and salt in large bowl. Cut in margarine until crumbly. Pat mixture over apples. Bake for 1 hour or until light brown. Serve warm with frozen yogurt. Yield: 8 servings.

Approx Per Serving: Cal 298; Prot 2 g; Carbo 48 g; Fiber 2 g;
   T Fat 12 g; 35% Calories from Fat; Chol 0 mg; Sod 205 mg.

For fluted fruit wheels, cut thin strips of rind evenly from stem end to blossom end of lemons, oranges and limes. Cut fruit into slices of desired thickness. To make twists, cut from one side to center and twist. For fans, cut fruit into slices, cutting to but not through bottom side; fan out slices.

Bananas Calypso

2 egg yolks
1/2 cup confectioners' sugar
1/2 cup light cream
1/2 teaspoon salt
2 teaspoons rum extract
2 egg whites

1 tablespoon margarine
1/2 cup packed dark brown sugar
1/4 teaspoon ground cloves
2 tablespoons grated orange rind
3/4 cup orange juice
8 bananas

Beat egg yolks in glass bowl until thick and lemon-colored. Add confectioners' sugar, cream and salt; mix well. Microwave on High for 1 minute and 45 seconds or until thickened, stirring every 30 seconds. Add rum extract gradually, beating until smooth. Beat egg whites until stiff peaks form. Fold into rum sauce; set aside. Microwave margarine in 3-quart glass bowl until melted. Add brown sugar, cloves, orange rind and orange juice; mix well. Microwave on High for 3 minutes. Peel bananas and slice lengthwise into thirds. Add to orange sauce, stirring to coat. Microwave for 3 minutes longer, stirring once. Serve with rum sauce. Yield: 8 servings.

Approx Per Serving: Cal 304; Prot 4 g; Carbo 54 g; Fiber 2 g;
T Fat 10 g; 25% Calories from Fat; Chol 69 mg; Sod 179 mg.

Biscuit Tortoni

24 vanilla wafers, crushed
3 cups light whipped topping
1/2 cup chopped almonds

1/4 cup drained chopped
maraschino cherries
2 teaspoons vanilla extract

Reserve 1/4 cup cookie crumbs. Fold remaining cookie crumbs into whipped topping. Fold in almonds, cherries and vanilla. Spoon into 12 paper-lined medium muffin cups. Sprinkle with reserved crumbs. Freeze until firm. Yield: 12 servings.

Approx Per Serving: Cal 106; Prot 1 g; Carbo 12 g; Fiber 1 g;
T Fat 6 g; 50% Calories from Fat; Chol 5 mg; Sod 31 mg.

For strawberry fans, select large firm strawberries with caps. Cut several parallel slices from the tip of each berry to just below the cap with a sharp knife. Spread slices gently to form fan.

Butterfinger Crunch

2 cups graham cracker crumbs
6 tablespoons margarine,
 softened
2 4-ounce packages vanilla
 instant pudding mix
2 cups low-fat milk

1/2 gallon frozen vanilla yogurt,
 softened
2 large Butterfinger candy bars,
 crushed
8 ounces light whipped topping

Mix cracker crumbs and margarine in 9x13-inch dish; press evenly into dish. Combine pudding mix and milk in bowl; mix until smooth. Let stand for 5 minutes. Blend in yogurt. Fold in 3/4 of the crushed candy bars. Spoon into prepared dish. Freeze for 30 minutes. Top with whipped topping and remaining crushed candy bars. Store in refrigerator. Yield: 12 servings.

Approx Per Serving: Cal 386; Prot 6 g; Carbo 59 g; Fiber 1 g;
     T Fat 15 g; 33% Calories from Fat; Chol 4 mg; Sod 408 mg.

Caramel Fondue

1 16-ounce package caramels

8 ounces light cream cheese

Melt caramels and cream cheese together in double boiler, stirring frequently. Pour into heated fondue pot. Serve with fresh fruit.
Yield: 10 servings.

Approx Per Serving: Cal 234; Prot 4 g; Carbo 37 g; Fiber 1 g;
     T Fat 9 g; 32% Calories from Fat; Chol 15 mg; Sod 232 mg.

Holiday Charlotte

2 3-ounce packages ladyfingers
2 teaspoons unflavored gelatin
1/4 cup cold pineapple juice
1/4 cup boiling pineapple juice
1/2 cup sugar

16 ounces light cream cheese,
 softened
12 ounces light whipped topping
1 15-ounce can crushed
 juice-pack pineapple, drained

Arrange ladyfingers over bottom and vertically around side of 8-inch springform pan. Soften gelatin in cold juice in bowl. Add boiling juice, stirring until gelatin dissolves. Cream sugar and cream cheese in mixer bowl until light and fluffy. Add gelatin mixture; mix well. Fold in whipped topping and pineapple. Pour into prepared pan. Chill overnight. Remove side of pan. Place on serving plate. Tie wide ribbon around dessert.
Yield: 8 servings.

Approx Per Serving: Cal 317; Prot 8 g; Carbo 43 g; Fiber 1 g;
     T Fat 13 g; 36% Calories from Fat; Chol 32 mg; Sod 340 mg.

Frozen Cherry Cheesecakes

8 ounces light cream cheese,
   softened
1/2 cup nonfat black cherry yogurt
2 tablespoons egg substitute

1/4 cup sugar
1 egg white, stiffly beaten
1 21-ounce can light cherry pie
   filling

Beat cream cheese, yogurt, egg substitute and sugar in mixer bowl until light and fluffy. Fold in egg white. Stir in half the pie filling. Spoon into paper-lined muffin cups. Freeze, covered, until firm. Remove paper-liners. Heat remaining pie filling in saucepan. Spoon over cheesecakes. Yield: 12 servings.

Approx Per Serving: Cal 107; Prot 3 g; Carbo 16 g; Fiber 0 g;
   T Fat 3 g; 28% Calories from Fat; Chol 11 mg; Sod 134 mg.

Chocolate-Cherry Delight

30 creme-filled chocolate
   sandwich cookies,
   crumbled
1/4 cup melted margarine

1/2 gallon frozen vanilla yogurt,
   softened
1 21-ounce can light cherry pie
   filling

Reserve 1/4 cup cookie crumbs. Combine remaining cookie crumbs with margarine in large bowl; mix well. Press over bottom of 9x13-inch dish. Chill for 10 to 15 minutes. Layer half the yogurt, pie filling, remaining yogurt and reserved crumbs in prepared dish. Chill, covered, for 2 hours. Cut into squares. Yield: 15 servings.

Approx Per Serving: Cal 210; Prot 3 g; Carbo 31 g; Fiber <1 g;
   T Fat 8 g; 35% Calories from Fat; Chol 0 mg; Sod 170 mg.

Cranberry Mousse

12 ounces light cream cheese,
   softened
2 tablespoons orange
   juice
1 1/2 tablespoons sugar

1 1/2 12-ounce jars cranberry-
   orange sauce
3 cups light whipped topping
1/4 cup fresh cranberries
12 mint leaves

Combine cream cheese, orange juice and sugar in mixer bowl. Beat until light and fluffy. Stir in cranberry-orange sauce. Fold in whipped topping. Spoon into stemmed dessert glasses. Chill until serving time. Garnish with fresh cranberries and mint leaves. Yield: 6 servings.

Approx Per Serving: Cal 357; Prot 6 g; Carbo 55 g; Fiber 3 g;
   T Fat 14 g; 33% Calories from Fat; Chol 32 mg; Sod 351 mg.

Lemon Creme Meringues

4 egg whites, at room
 temperature
1/4 teaspoon cream of tartar
1 cup superfine sugar
1 1/2 teaspoons almond extract
3/4 cup low-fat milk

1 4-ounce package lemon
 instant pudding mix
2 cups light whipped topping
1 lemon, sliced
2 kiwifruit, sliced
12 fresh mint leaves

Preheat oven to 225 degrees. Beat egg whites with cream of tartar in large mixer bowl until frothy. Add sugar very gradually, beating constantly for 10 to 15 minutes or until meringue forms stiff glossy peaks. Beat in almond extract. Spoon into 6 mounds on greased and floured baking sheet. Shape into cups with back of spoon. Bake for 1 hour. Turn off oven. Let meringues stand in closed oven until cool. Combine milk and pudding mix in bowl. Beat with rotary beater until smooth. Fold in whipped topping gently. Let stand for 5 minutes. Spoon lemon mixture into meringues. Garnish with lemon slices, kiwifruit slices and mint leaves. Yield: 6 servings.

Approx Per Serving: Cal 289; Prot 4 g; Carbo 63 g; Fiber 1 g;
 T Fat 4 g; 11% Calories from Fat; Chol 3 mg; Sod 177 mg.

Luscious Lemon Cream and Fruit

2 eggs
1/2 cup sugar
1/3 cup fresh lemon juice
1 tablespoon cornstarch
1/2 cup sugar

1/2 cup water
1 teaspoon vanilla extract
2 cups light whipped topping
6 cups mixed fresh fruit

Beat eggs, sugar and lemon juice in bowl until thickened. Mix cornstarch with 1/2 cup sugar in saucepan. Stir in water. Cook until thickened, stirring constantly. Stir a small amount of hot mixture into egg mixture; stir egg mixture into hot mixture. Cook over low heat until slightly thickened, stirring constantly. Stir in vanilla. Let stand until cool. Fold in whipped topping. Serve over fruit. Yield: 6 servings.

Approx Per Serving: Cal 450; Prot 6 g; Carbo 102 g; Fiber 3 g;
 T Fat 5 g; 10% Calories from Fat; Chol 71 mg; Sod 32 mg.

Serve coffee with a variety of interesting additions instead of dessert. Serve whipping cream, hot cream, cinnamon, cloves, vanilla, grated orange rind and chocolate.

Nectarine-Blueberry Shortcake

1 10-count can flaky biscuits
2 tablespoons melted margarine
1/4 cup sugar
1 teaspoon cinnamon
1 cup fresh blueberries

4 nectarines or peaches, peeled,
sliced
1/2 cup sugar
8 ounces light whipped topping

Preheat oven to 375 degrees. Separate each biscuit into 2 sections. Dip 1 side into margarine; dip into mixture of 1/4 cup sugar and cinnamon. Arrange 9 biscuit halves on greased baking sheet sugar side up with edges overlapping to form 8-inch ring. Place 1 biscuit in center. Repeat to form second ring. Bake for 11 to 14 minutes or until light brown; cool. Combine blueberries, nectarines and remaining 1/2 cup sugar in bowl; mix well. Layer biscuit ring, fruit mixture and whipped topping 1/2 at a time on serving plate. Slice to serve. Yield: 10 servings.

Approx Per Serving: Cal 191; Prot 2 g; Carbo 35 g; Fiber 2 g;
T Fat 5 g; 25% Calories from Fat; Chol 1 mg; Sod 277 mg.

Orange Terrine

2 4-serving packages sugar-free
lemon gelatin
1 1/2 cups boiling water
1 tablespoon grated orange rind
1 1/2 cups orange juice
12 ounces light whipped topping

1 10-ounce package frozen
strawberries in syrup, thawed
1 10-ounce package frozen
raspberries in syrup, thawed
2 teaspoons cornstarch
2 tablespoons fresh lemon juice

Dissolve gelatin in boiling water in bowl. Stir in orange rind and orange juice. Chill until thickened. Fold in 2 1/2 cups whipped topping. Spoon into 5x9-inch pan lined with waxed paper. Chill, covered, for 3 hours or until firm. Purée undrained berries in blender. Combine 1/2 cup purée with cornstarch in 2-quart saucepan. Stir in remaining purée and lemon juice. Bring to a boil over medium heat, stirring constantly. Cook for 1 minute, stirring constantly. Spoon into small bowl; cover surface with plastic wrap. Chill in refrigerator. Invert terrine onto plate; remove waxed paper. Cut into 1/2-inch slices. Spoon sauce onto serving plates. Place 1 slice terrine in sauce on each plate. Garnish with remaining whipped topping. Yield: 8 servings.

Approx Per Serving: Cal 102; Prot 2 g; Carbo 21 g; Fiber 2 g;
T Fat 2 g; 15% Calories from Fat; Chol 0 mg; Sod 56 mg.

Quick Peach Melba

1 10-ounce pound cake, cut into
    6 slices
1 10-ounce package frozen
    raspberries, thawed
1 1/2 pints frozen vanilla yogurt
1 10-ounce package frozen
    peaches, thawed
1 cup light whipped topping

Arrange cake slices on dessert plates. Top with raspberries, frozen yogurt, peaches and whipped topping. Yield: 6 servings.

Approx Per Serving: Cal 353; Prot 5 g; Carbo 58 g; Fiber 3 g;
     T Fat 10 g; 27% Calories from Fat; Chol 50 mg; Sod 188 mg.

Easy "Plum" Pudding

2 16-ounce packages fig
    newtons
3/4 cup chopped walnuts
1 cup milk
1 teaspoon vanilla extract
2 teaspoons rum extract
1/2 cup margarine, softened
2 eggs
2 tablespoons baking powder
1 tablespoon cinnamon
1/2 teaspoon cloves
3/4 teaspoon nutmeg

Break fig newtons into small pieces in bowl. Mix in walnuts. Add mixture of milk, vanilla and rum extract; mix well. Let stand for 15 minutes. Cream margarine in mixer bowl until light. Add eggs; beat until smooth. Beat for 1 minute longer. Add baking powder, cinnamon, cloves and nutmeg; beat for 1 minute. Add fig newton mixture gradually, beating constantly. Batter will be stiff. Spoon into greased and floured 2-quart pudding mold. Cover tightly. Place on rack or trivet in large saucepan. Add enough water to come halfway up side of mold. Steam, covered, for 2 1/2 hours or until cake tester inserted in pudding comes out clean. Place mold on wire rack; remove cover. Cool for 30 minutes. Remove from mold. Serve warm with frozen yogurt. May store steamed pudding, wrapped in foil, in refrigerator for up to 1 week. Reheat in foil in 325-degree oven for 1 hour. Yield: 12 servings.

Approx Per Serving: Cal 414; Prot 6 g; Carbo 57 g; Fiber <1 g;
     T Fat 19 g; 41% Calories from Fat; Chol 38 mg; Sod 544 mg.

Make a party sundae by arranging scoops of different flavors of ice cream in a large bowl. Serve with toppings such as crushed pineapple, coconut, nuts, mandarin oranges, chocolate syrup or strawberry preserves.

Snowball Dessert

2 envelopes unflavored gelatin
1 cup sugar
1 cup cold water
1　8-ounce can juice-pack
　　crushed pineapple
1　8-ounce can mandarin
　　oranges, drained

2 tablespoons lemon juice
16 ounces light whipped topping
1 cup flaked coconut
1　10-ounce angel food cake
1 cup confectioners' sugar
1 cup flaked coconut

Mix gelatin, sugar and water in saucepan. Let stand for several minutes. Heat until gelatin is dissolved. Add pineapple, oranges and lemon juice; mix well. Chill until partially set. Fold in half the whipped topping and 1 cup coconut. Tear cake into bite-sized pieces. Fold gently into gelatin mixture. Spoon into 9x13-inch dish. Combine confectioners' sugar, remaining whipped topping and 1/2 cup coconut in bowl; mix well. Spread over dessert. Sprinkle with remaining 1/2 cup coconut. Chill overnight. Yield: 12 servings.

Approx Per Serving: Cal 264; Prot 3 g; Carbo 53 g; Fiber 2 g;
　　T Fat 6 g; 18% Calories from Fat; Chol 0 mg; Sod 125 mg.

Spumoni Mold

1 quart pistachio ice milk,
　　softened
1/4 cup finely chopped
　　semisweet chocolate
1 quart frozen vanilla yogurt,
　　softened

1/2 cup chopped mixed candied
　　fruit
1 quart frozen chocolate yogurt,
　　softened
1/2 cup chopped pistachios
2 cups light whipped topping

Combine pistachio ice milk and semisweet chocolate in bowl; mix well. Spoon into 8-cup mold. Freeze until firm. Spoon mixture of vanilla yogurt and candied fruit over pistachio layer. Freeze until firm. Spoon mixture of chocolate yogurt and 1/2 cup pistachios over vanilla layer. Freeze until firm. Unmold onto serving plate. Pipe whipped topping rosettes around bottom of mold. Pipe additional rosettes from base to base across top. Garnish with additional chopped pistachios and semisweet chocolate shavings. Yield: 8 servings.

Approx Per Serving: Cal 329; Prot 7 g; Carbo 50 g; Fiber 1 g;
　　T Fat 12 g; 31% Calories from Fat; Chol 9 mg; Sod 113 mg.

Hot Apple Sundaes

2 tablespoons margarine
2 tablespoons light brown
  sugar
1 teaspoon lemon juice

2 large red apples, cut into
  1/4-inch slices
3 cups frozen vanilla yogurt
1/3 cup chopped walnuts

Melt margarine in skillet over medium heat. Stir in brown sugar and lemon juice; mix well. Add sliced apples. Cook for 10 minutes or until apples are tender. Scoop frozen yogurt into goblets. Top with apples, syrup and walnuts. Yield: 6 servings.

Approx Per Serving: Cal 168; Prot 3 g; Carbo 20 g; Fiber 1 g;
  T Fat 9 g; 47% Calories from Fat; Chol 0 mg; Sod 77 mg.

Waffle Sundaes

2 10-ounce packages
  quick-thaw frozen
  strawberries or raspberries in
  syrup, thawed
2 tablespoons cornstarch
2 tablespoons sugar

1/4 cup orange juice
8 frozen waffles
1 quart frozen vanilla yogurt
1 pint fresh strawberries or
  raspberries, sliced

Combine undrained strawberries, cornstarch and sugar in 2-quart saucepan; mix well. Cook mixture until thickened, stirring constantly. Strain into small bowl, discarding pulp and seed. Stir in orange juice. Chill, covered, for 2 hours or longer. Bake waffles using package directions. Place waffles on individual serving plates. Top with frozen yogurt, sliced strawberries and chilled sauce. Yield: 8 servings.

Approx Per Serving: Cal 225; Prot 4 g; Carbo 42 g; Fiber 3 g;
  T Fat 5 g; 19% Calories from Fat; Chol 20 mg; Sod 273 mg.

For a waffle buffet brunch, serve warm waffles with pitchers of plain and fruited syrups; bowls of fruit, preserves, nuts and chocolate chips; whipped cream and confectioners' sugar.

Frozen Malted Torte

1 cup finely crushed graham
  cracker crumbs
3 tablespoons sugar
1 teaspoon cinnamon
3 tablespoons melted margarine
2 tablespoons finely grated
  semisweet chocolate

¹/₂ gallon fudge marble frozen
  yogurt, softened
¹/₂ cup malted milk powder
4 ounces chocolate-covered
  malted milk balls, coarsely
  chopped

Combine cracker crumbs, sugar and cinnamon in bowl; mix well. Stir in margarine and chocolate. Press over bottom and halfway up side of greased springform pan. Blend frozen yogurt and malted milk powder in bowl. Spread in prepared pan. Sprinkle with chopped malted milk balls, pressing in lightly. Freeze, covered, for 4 hours or until firm. Loosen from side of pan with knife dipped in hot water. Place on serving plate; remove side of pan. Cut into wedges. Yield: 12 servings.

Approx Per Serving: Cal 241; Prot 5 g; Carbo 36 g; Fiber 1 g;
  T Fat 9 g; 33% Calories from Fat; Chol 2 mg; Sod 196 mg.

Tortilla Torte

1 cup semisweet chocolate chips
1 cup light sour cream
6 10-inch flour tortillas

1 tablespoon seedless red
  raspberry preserves

Melt chocolate chips in double boiler; remove from heat. Stir in sour cream. Cool to room temperature. Spread chocolate mixture over 5 tortillas. Spread preserves over 1 tortilla. Stack tortillas, placing tortilla with preserves in center of stack. Chill, covered, for 4 to 24 hours. Cut into wedges. Yield: 6 servings.

Approx Per Serving: Cal 337; Prot 5 g; Carbo 44 g; Fiber 2 g;
  T Fat 18 g; 45% Calories from Fat; Chol 16 mg; Sod 188 mg.

Yogurt Surprise

1 cup nonfat strawberry yogurt
  with strawberries
1 cup sliced strawberries

12 ounces light whipped topping
¹/₂ cup strawberry halves

Mix yogurt and sliced strawberries in bowl. Fold in whipped topping. Spoon into serving bowl. Garnish with strawberry halves. Yield: 6 servings.

Approx Per Serving: Cal 72; Prot 3 g; Carbo 11 g; Fiber 2 g;
  T Fat 2 g; 27% Calories from Fat; Chol 1 mg; Sod 30 mg.

Almond Cake

1 cup margarine, softened
1 1/3 cups sugar
3 ounces almond paste
1/2 teaspoon orange extract

6 eggs
1/2 cup all-purpose flour
2/3 teaspoon baking powder
1 1/2 cups apricot preserves

Preheat oven to 350 degrees. Cream margarine, sugar and almond paste in mixer bowl until light and fluffy. Add orange extract and eggs; mix well. Beat at high speed for 3 minutes. Add mixture of flour and baking powder; mix just until moistened. Spoon into greased and floured 7 or 8-inch bundt pan or springform pan. Bake for 40 minutes or until cake tests done. Cool in pan for 15 minutes. Remove to wire rack to cool completely. Bring preserves to a boil in saucepan; strain. Brush over top and side of cake until all glaze is absorbed. Yield: 12 servings.

Approx Per Serving: Cal 420; Prot 5 g; Carbo 58 g; Fiber 2 g;
    T Fat 20 g; 42% Calories from Fat; Chol 106 mg; Sod 236 mg.

Ambrosia Cake

2 1/2 cups all-purpose flour
1 teaspoon baking powder
1 teaspoon baking soda
1 cup sugar
1/4 teaspoon salt
1 cup chopped pecans
1/2 cup drained juice-pack
    pineapple tidbits

1 cup flaked coconut
1/2 cup drained maraschino
    cherries, coarsely chopped
2 tablespoons grated orange rind
2 eggs, beaten
1 cup buttermilk
3/4 cup oil

Preheat oven to 350 degrees. Mix flour, baking powder, baking soda, sugar and salt in bowl. Add pecans, pineapple tidbits, coconut, maraschino cherries and orange rind; mix well. Combine eggs, buttermilk and oil in bowl; mix well. Add to fruit mixture; mix well. Spoon into greased and floured 10-inch bundt pan. Bake for 45 to 50 minutes or until cake tests done. Cool in pan for 10 minutes. Remove to wire rack to cool completely. Yield: 16 servings.

Approx Per Serving: Cal 310; Prot 4 g; Carbo 35 g; Fiber 2 g;
    T Fat 18 g; 51% Calories from Fat; Chol 27 mg; Sod 132 mg.

Apple Dapple Cake

2 eggs	2 teaspoons vanilla extract
1 cup oil	1 cup pecans
2 cups sugar	3 cups chopped apples
3 cups all-purpose flour	1 cup packed brown sugar
1 teaspoon salt	1/4 cup margarine
1 teaspoon baking soda	1/4 cup milk

Preheat oven to 350 degrees. Combine eggs, oil and sugar in mixer bowl. Beat until smooth. Sift in flour, salt and baking soda. Mix until moistened. Stir in vanilla, pecans and apples. Spoon into greased 9x13-inch cake pan. Bake for 45 minutes. Combine brown sugar, margarine and milk in saucepan. Cook over medium heat for 2 1/2 minutes, stirring constantly. Pour over hot cake. Let stand until cool. Cut into squares. Yield: 15 servings.

Approx Per Serving: Cal 485; Prot 4 g; Carbo 65 g; Fiber 2 g;
    T Fat 24 g; 44% Calories from Fat; Chol 29 mg; Sod 251 mg.

Hot Applesauce Cakes

3 cups applesauce, heated	1 teaspoon allspice
2 cups sugar	1/2 teaspoon cloves
1 cup melted shortening	1 15-ounce package golden
1 teaspoon salt	raisins
4 1/2 cups sifted all-purpose flour	1 pound candied mixed fruit
4 teaspoons baking soda	3 cups chopped pecans
1 teaspoon nutmeg	1/2 16-ounce package red and
1 teaspoon cinnamon	green fruit-flavored gumdrops

Combine applesauce, sugar, shortening and salt in bowl; mix well. Let stand overnight. Preheat oven to 275 degrees. Sift flour, baking soda and spices into bowl. Add to applesauce mixture; mix well. Stir in raisins, candied fruit, pecans and gumdrops. Spoon into 3 greased loaf pans. Bake for 1 3/4 hours. Cool in pans for 10 minutes. Remove to wire rack to cool completely. Yield: 36 servings.

Approx Per Serving: Cal 326; Prot 3 g; Carbo 53 g; Fiber 2 g;
    T Fat 13 g; 34% Calories from Fat; Chol 0 mg; Sod 155 mg.

Holiday Carrot Cake

2 cups sugar
1¹/₂ cups oil
4 eggs
3 cups self-rising flour
1¹/₂ teaspoons cinnamon

2 cups shredded carrots
1 10-ounce jar maraschino
     cherries, finely chopped
1¹/₂ cups chopped walnuts
¹/₂ 3-ounce can flaked coconut

Preheat oven to 350 degrees. Combine sugar and oil in large mixer bowl. Beat until light. Add eggs 1 at a time, beating well after each addition. Add mixture of flour and cinnamon gradually, beating until smooth. Stir in carrots, maraschino cherries, walnuts and coconut. Pour into greased and floured bundt pan. Bake for 1¹/₄ hours or until cake tests done. Cool in pan for 10 minutes. Invert onto wire rack to cool completely. Yield: 16 servings.

Approx Per Serving: Cal 490; Prot 6 g; Carbo 52 g; Fiber 2 g;
     T Fat 30 g; 54% Calories from Fat; Chol 53 mg; Sod 277 mg.

Eggnogging Chocolate Cake

1¹/₄ cups water
¹/₃ cup oil
³/₄ cup egg substitute
1 2-layer package German
     chocolate cake mix

2 cups eggnog
1 cup packed light brown sugar
1 cup sugar
1 cup chopped pecans

Preheat oven to 350 degrees. Beat water, oil, egg substitute and cake mix in mixer bowl at medium speed for 2 minutes. Pour into 10x15-inch cake pan sprayed with nonstick cooking spray. Bake for 28 minutes. Mix eggnog, brown sugar and sugar in microwave-safe bowl. Microwave on Medium for 10 minutes. Pour into 2-quart saucepan. Stir in pecans. Cook over medium heat, stirring frequently. Punch several holes in cake with wooden spoon. Pour hot eggnog mixture over cake. Chill in refrigerator for 10 to 15 minutes. Serve warm. Yield: 35 servings.

Approx Per Serving: Cal 178; Prot 2 g; Carbo 28 g; Fiber <1 g;
     T Fat 7 g; 34% Calories from Fat; Chol 9 mg; Sod 158 mg.

Make a Jack-O'-Lantern cake for Halloween by placing 2 bundt cakes bottom to bottom and matching the ribs. Decorate with colored frosting.

Cranberry Upside-Down Cakes

1¹/₃ cups sugar
4 cups fresh cranberries
5 egg yolks
1¹/₂ cups sugar
³/₄ cup water
¹/₂ cup oil
2 teaspoons grated lemon rind

2 teaspoons vanilla extract
2 cups all-purpose flour
1 tablespoon baking powder
1 teaspoon salt
7 egg whites
¹/₂ teaspoon cream of tartar

Preheat oven to 350 degrees. Sprinkle ¹/₃ cup sugar in each of 2 greased 8x8-inch cake pans. Arrange cranberries in prepared pans. Sprinkle each with ¹/₃ cup sugar. Bake, covered with foil, for 30 minutes. Cool. Combine egg yolks, 1¹/₂ cups sugar, water, oil, lemon rind and vanilla in mixer bowl; mix well. Add mixture of flour, baking powder and salt; mix well. Beat egg whites with cream of tartar in mixer bowl until soft peaks form. Fold gently into batter. Spoon over cranberries. Bake for 35 minutes or until layers test done. Cool in pans for 5 minutes. Invert onto wire rack. Serve with whipped topping. Yield: 12 servings.

Approx Per Serving: Cal 390; Prot 5 g; Carbo 67 g; Fiber 2 g;
T Fat 12 g; 27% Calories from Fat; Chol 89 mg; Sod 294 mg.

Mint and Fudge Cake

1 2-layer package white cake mix
2 tablespoons non-alcholic green Crème de Menthe syrup
1 12-ounce can chocolate fudge sauce

8 ounces light whipped topping
2 tablespoons non-alcholic green Crème de Menthe syrup

Preheat oven to 350 degrees. Prepare and bake cake mix using package directions for 9x13-inch cake pan, adding 2 tablespoons Crème de Menthe syrup to batter. Cool in pan. Spread with fudge sauce. Beat whipped topping and 2 tablespoons Crème de Menthe syrup in bowl. Spread over cake. Garnish with chocolate sprinkles. Yield: 15 servings.

Approx Per Serving: Cal 263; Prot 2 g; Carbo 50 g; Fiber 1 g;
T Fat 6 g; 20% Calories from Fat; Chol 1 mg; Sod 240 mg.

Easy Fruity Crown Cake

1 1-layer package yellow cake
   mix
1 egg, beaten
1/2 cup water

1 9-ounce can vanilla pudding
2 cups sliced strawberries
1 cup sliced kiwifruit
1/2 cup chopped pecans

Preheat oven to 350 degrees. Combine cake mix, egg and water in bowl; mix well. Pour into greased and floured Marion pan. Bake for 10 minutes or until golden brown. Invert onto cake plate while warm; cool. Fill center with vanilla pudding. Layer with strawberries, kiwifruit and pecans. Chill before serving. Yield: 8 servings.

Approx Per Serving: Cal 428; Prot 5 g; Carbo 73 g; Fiber 4 g;
    T Fat 14 g; 28% Calories from Fat; Chol 27 mg; Sod 473 mg.

Molasses and Spice Gingerbread

2 3/4 cups sifted all-purpose flour
3/4 cup plus 2 tablespoons sugar
2 teaspoons baking powder
1 teaspoon baking soda
1 tablespoon cinnamon
1 tablespoon ginger
1/4 teaspoon cloves

1 teaspoon salt
3/4 cup plus 2 tablespoons
   shortening
1 cup molasses
1 cup very hot water
2 eggs
1/4 cup confectioners' sugar

Preheat oven to 350 degrees. Sift flour, sugar, baking powder, baking soda, cinnamon, ginger, cloves and salt together in bowl. Cut in shortening until crumbly. Mix molasses with hot water in small bowl. Stir into flour mixture; mix until smooth. Add eggs; mix well. Spoon into 2 greased and floured 8x8-inch cake pans. Bake for 35 minutes or until gingerbread tests done. Let stand until cool. Place doily on top of gingerbread. Sprinkle with confectioners' sugar. Remove doily gently. Yield: 12 servings.

Approx Per Serving: Cal 365; Prot 4 g; Carbo 52 g; Fiber 1 g;
    T Fat 16 g; 39% Calories from Fat; Chol 36 mg; Sod 317 mg.

A centerpiece does not have to be flowers. An element of the menu can serve as a beautiful focus for the center of the table. Try a festively decorated cake on a cake stand, a basket or cornucopia of fresh fruit with paring knives, a holiday bombe or Charlotte, soup or cider in a pumpkin, a bread wreath centered with a candle, or a pineapple studded with canapés.

Mandarin Cake

2 11-ounce cans mandarin
   oranges
2 cups all-purpose flour
2 cups sugar
2 teaspoons vanilla extract
2 teaspoons baking soda

2 eggs
1 teaspoon salt
1 cup chopped walnuts
³/4 cup packed light brown sugar
3 tablespoons milk
3 tablespoons margarine

Preheat oven to 350 degrees. Combine undrained mandarin oranges, flour, sugar, vanilla, baking soda, eggs, salt and walnuts in mixer bowl; beat until well mixed. Pour into ungreased 9x13-inch cake pan. Bake for 30 to 35 minutes or until cake tests done. Cool in pan. Pierce with fork or toothpick. Combine brown sugar, milk and margarine in saucepan. Bring to a boil, stirring occasionally. Pour over cake. Yield: 12 servings.

Approx Per Serving: Cal 405; Prot 5 g; Carbo 76 g; Fiber 2 g; T Fat 10 g; 22% Calories from Fat; Chol 36 mg; Sod 374 mg.

Popcorn Cake

4 quarts popped popcorn
2 2-ounce packages "M & M's"
   Plain Chocolate Candies
2 2-ounce packages "M & M's"
   Peanut Chocolate Candies

1 cup chopped pecans
1¹/2 pounds marshmallows
¹/4 cup oil
¹/2 cup margarine

Combine popcorn, candies and pecans in large bowl; mix well. Combine marshmallows, oil and margarine in saucepan. Cook until marshmallows and margarine are melted, stirring frequently. Pour over popcorn mixture; mix well. Press into angel food cake pan to mold. Invert onto serving plate. Yield: 12 servings.

Approx Per Serving: Cal 489; Prot 5 g; Carbo 68 g; Fiber 3 g; T Fat 24 g; 42% Calories from Fat; Chol 0 mg; Sod 154 mg.

The centerpiece for your table can carry out the theme of the party or holiday. Arrange small kitchen gadgets in a basket for a bridal shower or luncheon or gaily-colored shakers in a megaphone for a football buffet. Decorate a branch with symbols of the season such as hearts, shamrocks, pumpkins or eggs. Make a construction-paper head to attach to a pineapple turkey in a bed of fall leaves.

Peachy Apple Pie

1 recipe 2-crust pie pastry
1   21-ounce can light apple pie
    filling
1   15-ounce can sliced
    juice-pack cling peaches,
    drained
1/2 teaspoon apple pie spice
2 eggs
2 tablespoons lemon juice
1/3 cup sugar
4 ounces light cream cheese,
    softened

Preheat oven to 350 degrees. Fit half the pastry into deep-dish pie plate. Spoon mixture of pie filling, peaches and apple pie spice into prepared pie plate. Combine eggs, lemon juice and sugar in 1-quart saucepan; mix well. Cook over medium heat until thickened. Add cream cheese. Stir until blended. Pour over fruit. Top with remaining pastry. Bake for 45 to 50 minutes or until golden brown. Yield: 8 servings.

Approx Per Serving: Cal 371; Prot 6 g; Carbo 49 g; Fiber 1 g;
      T Fat 17 g; 42% Calories from Fat; Chol 61 mg; Sod 391 mg.

Fruit Stand Pie

2 Granny Smith apples, sliced
1 1/2 cups blackberries
1 1/2 cups raspberries
1 1/2 cups rhubarb
1 1/3 cups unsweetened apple
    juice
1/2 cup packed light brown sugar
2 tablespoons honey
1 teaspoon cloves
1 teaspoon grated lemon rind
3 tablespoons cornstarch
1 unbaked 9-inch pie shell

Preheat oven to 375 degrees. Combine first 9 ingredients in saucepan. Cook until apples are tender, stirring frequently. Stir in mixture of cornstarch and a small amount of water. Cook until thickened. Pour into pie shell. Bake for 35 minutes. Yield: 8 servings.

Approx Per Serving: Cal 271; Prot 2 g; Carbo 50 g; Fiber 5 g;
      T Fat 8 g; 25% Calories from Fat; Chol 0 mg; Sod 147 mg.

Lemonade Pie

1   6-ounce can frozen lemonade
    concentrate, thawed
8 ounces light whipped
    topping
1 1/2 pints frozen vanilla yogurt,
    softened
1   8-inch chocolate crumb pie
    shell

Combine first 3 ingredients in bowl; mix well. Pour into pie shell. Freeze until serving time. Yield: 8 servings.

Approx Per Serving: Cal 212; Prot 2 g; Carbo 34 g; Fiber <1 g;
      T Fat 7 g; 30% Calories from Fat; Chol 0 mg; Sod 123 mg.

Peach Petal Pie

1 package refrigerator sugar
   cookie dough
1 20-ounce can light peach pie
   filling

1 teaspoon sugar
Dash of cinnamon

Preheat oven to 350 degrees. Cut dough into ten ¼-inch slices. Heat pie filling in saucepan. Spoon into 8-inch pie plate. Arrange dough slices over pie filling, overlapping slices around edge. Sprinkle with mixture of sugar and cinnamon. Bake for 35 to 40 minutes or until cookie dough is brown. Serve warm with ice cream. Yield: 6 servings.

Approx Per Serving: Cal 611; Prot 8 g; Carbo 779 g; Fiber 0 g;
     T Fat 23 g; 6% Calories from Fat; Chol 0 mg; Sod 551 mg.

Sensational Double-Layer Pumpkin Pie

3 ounces light cream cheese,
   softened
1 tablespoon cold milk
1 tablespoon sugar
1½ cups light whipped topping
1 9-inch graham cracker pie
   shell

1 cup cold low-fat milk
2 4-ounce packages vanilla
   instant pudding mix
1 16-ounce can pumpkin
1 teaspoon cinnamon
½ teaspoon ginger
¼ teaspoon cloves

Combine first 3 ingredients in bowl; beat with wire whisk until smooth. Fold in 1½ cups whipped topping. Spread in pie shell. Combine remaining 1 cup milk and pudding mix in bowl; beat with wire whisk for 1 to 2 minutes or until well blended. Let stand for 3 minutes. Beat in pumpkin, cinnamon, ginger and cloves. Spread over cream cheese mixture. Chill for 2 hours. Garnish with additional whipped topping and nuts. Yield: 8 servings.

Approx Per Serving: Cal 399; Prot 5 g; Carbo 64 g; Fiber 2 g;
     T Fat 15 g; 33% Calories from Fat; Chol 9 mg; Sod 508 mg.

Strawberry Parfait Pie

1 3-ounce package strawberry
   gelatin
1 cup boiling water

2 cups frozen vanilla yogurt
1 to 2 cups sliced strawberries
1 baked 9-inch pie shell

Mix gelatin and boiling water in bowl. Stir in yogurt until well blended. Fold in strawberries. Pour into pie shell. Chill until set. Yield: 8 servings.

Approx Per Serving: Cal 199; Prot 4 g; Carbo 29 g; Fiber 2 g;
     T Fat 8 g; 37% Calories from Fat; Chol 0 mg; Sod 187 mg.

Candy & Cookies

Almond Clusters

2 tablespoons margarine
¼ cup milk
1   18-ounce package creamy
    frosting mix

1½ cups slivered almonds

Melt margarine with milk in saucepan over low heat; remove from heat. Stir in frosting mix. Cook over low heat for 1 to 2 minutes or until smooth and glossy, stirring constantly. Stir in slivered almonds. Drop by teaspoonfuls onto waxed paper. Let stand until firm. Add 2 additional teaspoons milk if using chocolate fudge frosting mix. Yield: 12 servings.

Approx Per Serving: Cal 322; Prot 5 g; Carbo 38 g; Fiber 2 g;
    T Fat 17 g; 47% Calories from Fat; Chol 1 mg; Sod 229 mg.

Baby Ruth Candy

2 cups semisweet chocolate
    chips
½ cup chunky peanut butter

1   7-ounce jar marshmallow
    creme
1 cup chopped salted peanuts

Melt chocolate chips and peanut butter in double boiler over hot water, stirring occasionally. Remove from heat. Add marshmallow creme and peanuts; beat until well mixed. Pour into foil-lined 8x8-inch glass dish. Cool completely. Cut into squares. Yield: 12 servings.

Approx Per Serving: Cal 316; Prot 7 g; Carbo 34 g; Fiber 2 g;
    T Fat 20 g; 53% Calories from Fat; Chol 0 mg; Sod 108 mg.

Candy Hash

4 cups Cap'n Crunch's Crunch
  Berries cereal
2 cups dry-roasted peanuts
2 cups slivered almonds

2 cups miniature marshmallows
1 pound white chocolate candy
  coating

Mix cereal, peanuts, almonds and marshmallows in large bowl. Melt candy coating in saucepan over low heat, stirring constantly. Pour over cereal mixture; mix well. Spread on baking sheet. Let stand until firm. Break into small pieces. Store in airtight container. Yield: 10 servings.

Approx Per Serving: Cal 654; Prot 16 g; Carbo 58 g; Fiber 5 g;
    T Fat 44 g; 57% Calories from Fat; Chol 10 mg; Sod 382 mg.

Cherry Bings

2 cups sugar
2/3 cup evaporated skim milk
12 large marshmallows
1/2 cup margarine
1 cup cherry baking chips
1 teaspoon vanilla extract

2 cups semisweet chocolate chips
3/4 cup peanut butter
1 tablespoon margarine
10 ounces salted peanuts,
  crushed

Bring sugar, evaporated milk, marshmallows and 1/2 cup margarine to a boil in saucepan over medium heat, stirring constantly. Cook for 5 minutes; remove from heat. Stir in cherry chips and vanilla. Pour into greased 9x13-inch dish. Melt chocolate chips in double boiler. Add peanut butter, 1 tablespoon margarine and peanuts; mix well. Spread over cherry layer. Chill until firm. Cut into small squares. May substitute chopped candied cherries for cherry chips if preferred. Yield: 32 servings.

Approx Per Serving: Cal 249; Prot 5 g; Carbo 26 g; Fiber 2 g;
    T Fat 15 g; 53% Calories from Fat; Chol <1 mg; Sod 115 mg.

Fashion napkins into festive roses for holiday table settings. Unfold each napkin completely and fold all 4 corners to center. Repeat process 2 additional times. Turn napkin over and fold 4 points to center once more. Hold points together firmly in center of napkin with finger. Pull 1 petal out and up from underneath each corner. Pull 1 petal out and up from between each of first 4 petals. Pull remaining 4 petals out and up.

Chocolate Clouds

3 egg whites, at room
   temperature
1/8 teaspoon cream of tartar
3/4 cup sugar

1 teaspoon vanilla extract
2 tablespoons baking cocoa
13/4 cups semisweet chocolate
   chunks

Preheat oven to 300 degrees. Line baking sheet with baking parchment. Beat egg whites with cream of tartar in mixer bowl until soft peaks form. Add sugar and vanilla gradually, beating until stiff peaks form. Sift baking cocoa over meringue; fold in gently. Fold in chocolate chunks. Drop by heaping tablespoonfuls onto prepared baking sheet. Bake for 35 to 45 minutes or just until dry. Peel carefully off parchment. Cool on wire rack. Store, covered, at room temperature. Yield: 10 servings.

Approx Per Serving: Cal 216; Prot 2 g; Carbo 33 g; Fiber 1 g;
   T Fat 11 g; 41% Calories from Fat; Chol 0 mg; Sod 20 mg.

Chocolate Mousse Balls

16 ounces milk chocolate
8 ounces light whipped topping

2/3 cup crushed vanilla wafers

Melt chocolate in saucepan over low heat, stirring frequently. Cool to room temperature. Beat in whipped topping. Chill, covered, for 1 hour. Shape into 1-inch balls. Roll in wafer crumbs. Place in paper petits fours cups. Chill until serving time. Yield: 24 servings.

Approx Per Serving: Cal 113; Prot 1 g; Carbo 13 g; Fiber 1 g;
   T Fat 7 g; 51% Calories from Fat; Chol 6 mg; Sod 25 mg.

Coconut Peaks

1/4 cup margarine
2 cups confectioners' sugar
1/4 cup evaporated skim milk
3 cups flaked coconut

1 teaspoon vanilla extract
1/2 cup semisweet chocolate chips
2 tablespoons margarine

Melt 1/4 cup margarine in saucepan over medium heat. Cook until golden brown, stirring constantly; remove from heat. Add next 4 ingredients; mix well. Drop by spoonfuls onto plate. Chill until firm enough to shape into cones with flattened bottoms; place in paper bonbon cups. Melt chocolate chips with 2 tablespoons margarine in saucepan over low heat, stirring constantly. Drizzle melted chocolate mixture over tops of cones and allow to run down sides of cones to resemble mountains. Yield: 8 servings.

Approx Per Serving: Cal 380; Prot 2 g; Carbo 49 g; Fiber 4 g;
   T Fat 22 g; 49% Calories from Fat; Chol <1 mg; Sod 117 mg.

Fruit Logs

2¹/₂ cups mixed chopped dried
   fruits such as pitted prunes,
   pears, apricots and apples
1¹/₄ cups figs
1 cup flaked coconut

¹/₂ cup baking cocoa
2 tablespoons orange juice
2 tablespoons honey
1 cup semisweet chocolate chips
1 tablespoon shortening

Combine mixed dried fruits, figs, coconut and baking cocoa in food processor container. Process with metal blade until chopped. Combine with orange juice and honey in large bowl; mix well. Divide into 2 portions. Shape each portion into 8-inch roll. Wrap in plastic wrap. Chill overnight. Microwave chocolate chips and shortening on High in glass dish for 30 seconds or until melted. Drizzle half the chocolate over fruit logs on waxed paper-lined tray. Cool slightly. Drizzle with remaining chocolate; draw spatula through chocolate to form texture of bark. Chill until chocolate is set. Store at room temperature in airtight container. Cut into slices. May shape into 1¹/₄-inch balls and roll in chopped nuts or confectioners' sugar if preferred. Yield: 10 servings.

Approx Per Serving: Cal 269; Prot 3 g; Carbo 48 g; Fiber 5 g;
   T Fat 11 g; 32% Calories from Fat; Chol 0 mg; Sod 13 mg.

Filled Meringues

3 egg whites
¹/₄ teaspoon cream of tartar
¹/₄ teaspoon almond extract
1 cup sugar

8 ounces soft light cream cheese
   with strawberries
1 cup light strawberry preserves

Preheat oven to 300 degrees. Beat egg whites, cream of tartar and almond extract at medium speed in mixer bowl until soft peaks form. Add sugar gradually, beating at high speed until stiff. Drop by tablespoonfuls 3 inches apart onto baking sheet lined with baking parchment. Make well in center with spoon, building up sides. Bake for 20 minutes. Turn off oven. Let meringues stand in closed oven for 30 minutes. Fill with cream cheese and preserves. Yield: 12 servings.

Approx Per Serving: Cal 168; Prot 2 g; Carbo 25 g; Fiber 0 g;
   T Fat 7 g; 36% Calories from Fat; Chol 0 mg; Sod 103 mg.

Save coffee cans and cover them with bright contact paper. Use them as airtight containers for delivering holiday candy treats.

Chocolate-Covered Orange Slices

1   16-ounce package miniature
    candied orange slices
2 ounces paraffin

1 cup semisweet chocolate chips
2 ounces white chocolate candy
    coating

Place toothpick in each orange slice. Melt paraffin with chocolate chips in double boiler. Dip orange slices into chocolate. Place on waxed paper-lined surface. Repeat process. Melt white chocolate in double boiler. Dip one end of each orange slice in white chocolate with toothpick. Place on waxed paper-lined surface. Let stand until firm. Place in paper bonbon cups. Yield: 12 servings.

Approx Per Serving: Cal 231; Prot 1 g; Carbo 43 g; Fiber 1 g;
    T Fat 7 g; 25% Calories from Fat; Chol 1 mg; Sod 33 mg.
    Nutritional information does not include paraffin.

Peanut Butter-Marshmallow Candy

2 cups marshmallow creme
1 cup peanut butter
1   2-pound package
    confectioners' sugar

8 ounces semisweet chocolate
2 ounces paraffin

Combine marshmallow creme and peanut butter in bowl; mix well. Stir in enough confectioners' sugar to make stiff mixture. Shape into balls. Chill in refrigerator. Melt chocolate with paraffin in double boiler. Dip candy into chocolate with toothpick. Place on waxed paper-lined surface. Let stand until firm. Yield: 36 servings.

Approx Per Serving: Cal 236; Prot 3 g; Carbo 47 g; Fiber <1 g;
    T Fat 6 g; 21% Calories from Fat; Chol 0 mg; Sod 38 mg.

Peppermint Pecans

1 cup sugar
1/4 cup water
1 tablespoon light corn syrup
1 teaspoon peppermint extract

1 tablespoon (heaping)
    marshmallow creme
4 cups pecan halves

Bring sugar, water and corn syrup to a boil in saucepan. Boil for 1 minute; remove from heat. Add peppermint extract and marshmallow creme; blend well. Add pecans; stir until coated. Drop onto waxed paper; separate into clusters. Cool. Store in airtight container. Yield: 16 servings.

Approx Per Serving: Cal 235; Prot 2 g; Carbo 19 g; Fiber 2 g;
    T Fat 18 g; 66% Calories from Fat; Chol 0 mg; Sod 2 mg.

Pineapple Pecans

3¹/₃ cups sugar
³/₄ cup pineapple juice

6 cups pecan halves
1 cup confectioners' sugar

Combine sugar and pineapple juice in heavy 2-quart saucepan. Cook over low heat until sugar dissolves, stirring constantly. Cook over medium heat to 234 to 240 degrees on candy thermometer, soft-ball stage, stirring constantly; remove from heat. Add pecans; stir until coated. Sprinkle confectioners' sugar in thin layer on waxed paper-lined tray. Spread pecans in single layer on prepared tray; toss until pecans are coated. Let stand until cool. Store in airtight container. Yield: 24 servings.

Approx Per Serving: Cal 310; Prot 2 g; Carbo 40 g; Fiber 2 g;
     T Fat 20 g; 50% Calories from Fat; Chol 0 mg; Sod 1 mg.

Easy Popcorn Balls

1 cup packed light brown sugar
8 cups miniature marshmallows

¹/₂ cup margarine
3 quarts popped popcorn

Combine brown sugar, marshmallows and margarine in saucepan. Cook over low heat until marshmallows are melted, stirring constantly. Pour over popcorn in large bowl; mix lightly. Shape into 20 balls. Place on waxed paper. Let stand until firm. Store in airtight container. Yield: 20 servings.

Approx Per Serving: Cal 182; Prot 1 g; Carbo 35 g; Fiber 1 g;
     T Fat 5 g; 23% Calories from Fat; Chol 0 mg; Sod 80 mg.

Miraculous Pralines

1 cup evaporated skim milk
1 1-pound package light brown
    sugar

2 cups broken pecans
1 teaspoon vanilla extract
2 tablespoons melted margarine

Combine evaporated milk and brown sugar in glass bowl; mix well. Microwave on High for 8 to 12 minutes or until mixture boils. Stir in pecans, vanilla and margarine. Drop by spoonfuls onto foil-lined tray. Let stand until firm. Yield: 12 servings.

Approx Per Serving: Cal 307; Prot 3 g; Carbo 43 g; Fiber 1 g;
     T Fat 15 g; 43% Calories from Fat; Chol 1 mg; Sod 64 mg.

Iced Pretzels

2 egg whites
1/4 teaspoon cream of tartar
1/2 teaspoon vanilla extract

1 cup confectioners' sugar, sifted
8 ounces 3-ring pretzels
1/2 cup colored sugar sprinkles

Beat egg whites with cream of tartar at high speed in mixer bowl until soft peaks form. Add vanilla. Add confectioners' sugar 1 tablespoon at a time, beating until stiff peaks form. Dip tops of pretzels into icing. Place iced side up on wire rack. Decorate with sugar sprinkles. Let stand until firm. Store in airtight container. Yield: 16 servings.

Approx Per Serving: Cal 112; Prot 2 g; Carbo 25 g; Fiber <1 g;
    T Fat <1 g; 4% Calories from Fat; Chol 0 mg; Sod 235 mg.

Walnut Bonbons

8 ounces light cream cheese,
    softened
7 cups confectioners' sugar

1 teaspoon walnut extract
1 1/2 cups walnut halves
2 cups flaked coconut

Combine cream cheese, confectioners' sugar and walnut extract in bowl; mix well. Shape a small amount of cream cheese mixture around each walnut half; roll in coconut to coat. Place in paper bonbon cups. Chill until set. Serve at room temperature. Yield: 20 servings.

Approx Per Serving: Cal 269; Prot 3 g; Carbo 47 g; Fiber 1 g;
    T Fat 9 g; 29% Calories from Fat; Chol 6 mg; Sod 67 mg.

White Chocolate Crunch

1 14-ounce package
    Honeycomb cereal
1 12-ounce package pretzels
12 ounces mixed nuts

2 pounds white chocolate candy
    coating
1/2 cup candy sprinkles

Mix cereal, pretzels and nuts in very large bowl. Melt white chocolate in double boiler over hot water. Pour over cereal; stir to coat well. Spread on waxed paper. Sprinkle with candy sprinkles. Cool completely. Store in airtight container. Yield: 10 servings.

Approx Per Serving: Cal 980; Prot 18 g; Carbo 131 g; Fiber 7 g;
    T Fat 50 g; 43% Calories from Fat; Chol 19 mg; Sod 921 mg.

Apricot Cookies

1 cup margarine, softened
1/2 cup sugar
2 cups all-purpose flour
Salt to taste
1   21-ounce can apricot or peach
   pie filling

1/2 cup light apricot preserves
1/3 cup margarine softened
1/4 cup sugar
1/4 cup packed light brown sugar
1/4 teaspoon salt
3/4 cup all-purpose flour

Preheat oven to 350 degrees. Cream 1 cup margarine and 1/2 cup sugar in mixer bowl until light and fluffy. Add 2 cups flour and salt to taste; mix until crumbly. Press into greased 11x16-inch baking pan. Bake for 10 minutes. Cool slightly. Spread with mixture of pie filling and preserves. Combine remaining ingredients in small bowl; mix well. Sprinkle over filling. Bake for 30 to 35 minutes. Cut into bars. Yield: 12 servings.

Approx Per Serving: Cal 415; Prot 3 g; Carbo 56 g; Fiber 1 g;
   T Fat 21 g; 44% Calories from Fat; Chol 0 mg; Sod 309 mg.

Brownie Bites

1   15-ounce package brownie
   mix
1/3 cup hot water

1/4 cup oil
1 egg
48 miniature peanut butter cups

Preheat oven to 350 degrees. Combine brownie mix, water, oil and egg in mixer bowl; mix well. Fill paper-lined miniature muffin cups 1/2 full. Press 1 candy cup into batter in each cup. Bake for 15 to 20 minutes or until brownies are set. Remove to wire rack to cool. Yield: 16 servings.

Approx Per Serving: Cal 274; Prot 5 g; Carbo 32 g; Fiber 1 g;
   T Fat 14 g; 46% Calories from Fat; Chol 15 mg; Sod 145 mg.

Chocolate Toffee Crescent Bars

1   8-count can crescent rolls
1 cup packed light brown sugar
1 cup margarine

1 1/2 cups chopped pecans
1 cup chocolate chips

Preheat oven to 375 degrees. Separate roll dough into rectangles. Press over bottom of 10x15-inch baking pan; press perforations to seal. Bring brown sugar and margarine to a boil in saucepan, stirring constantly. Boil for 1 minute. Pour over dough. Sprinkle with pecans. Bake for 14 minutes or until golden brown. Sprinkle with chocolate chips. Let stand for 2 minutes; swirl chocolate over top. Let stand until cool. Cut into bars. Yield: 16 servings.

Approx Per Serving: Cal 344; Prot 2 g; Carbo 30 g; Fiber 1 g;
   T Fat 26 g; 64% Calories from Fat; Chol 0 mg; Sod 258 mg.

Cocoa Sandies

1 cup margarine, softened
1¼ cups confectioners' sugar
1½ teaspoons vanilla extract
½ cup baking cocoa

1¾ cups all-purpose flour
1½ cups confectioners' sugar
2 tablespoons baking cocoa
¼ cup low-fat milk

Preheat oven to 300 degrees. Cream margarine, 1¼ cups confectioners' sugar and vanilla in mixer bowl until light and fluffy. Add ½ cup baking cocoa; beat well. Add flour gradually, beating until smooth. Roll dough to ½-inch thickness on lightly floured surface. Cut with 2½-inch heart or star-shaped cookie cutter. Place on ungreased cookie sheet. Bake for 20 minutes or just until firm. Cool on cookie sheet for several minutes. Remove to wire rack to cool completely. Combine remaining 1½ cups confectioners' sugar and 2 tablespoons baking cocoa in small bowl; mix well. Stir in enough milk to make of glaze consistency. Dip half of each cookie into glaze. Place on wire rack. Let stand until glaze is set. Yield: 8 servings.

Approx Per Serving: Cal 486; Prot 5 g; Carbo 66 g; Fiber 3 g;
    T Fat 24 g; 44% Calories from Fat; Chol 1 mg; Sod 274 mg.

Cookie Press Gingersnaps

¾ cup margarine, softened
¾ cup packed light brown sugar
¾ cup molasses
1 egg
3 cups sifted all-purpose flour
1½ teaspoons baking soda

1 teaspoon cinnamon
1 teaspoon ginger
¼ teaspoon cloves
¼ teaspoon salt
¼ cup sugar sprinkles

Preheat oven to 375 degrees. Cream margarine and brown sugar in mixer bowl until light and fluffy. Blend in molasses and egg. Sift in flour, baking soda, cinnamon, ginger, cloves and salt; mix well. Spoon into cookie press. Press onto ungreased cookie sheet. Sprinkle with sugar sprinkles. Bake for 8 minutes or until golden brown. Remove to wire rack to cool.
Yield: 16 servings.

Approx Per Serving: Cal 252; Prot 3 g; Carbo 40 g; Fiber 1 g;
    T Fat 9 g; 32% Calories from Fat; Chol 13 mg; Sod 223 mg.

To add colorful sparkle to your holiday dessert tray, roll refrigerator cookie dough into a log and coat in a mixture of candied fruit and chopped almonds or walnuts. Refrigerate until firm, then slice and bake according to package directions.

Orange Slice Bar Cookies

1 pound candied orange slices
2 cups sifted all-purpose flour
1/2 teaspoon salt
3 cups packed light brown sugar

4 eggs, beaten
1 cup chopped pecans
1 teaspoon vanilla extract
1 cup sugar

Preheat oven to 350 degrees. Chop orange slices. Toss with flour and salt in bowl. Add brown sugar, eggs, pecans and vanilla; mix well. Spread in greased 10x15-inch baking pan. Bake for 35 minutes; cool in pan. Cut into 1x3-inch bars; roll in sugar. Yield: 16 servings.

Approx Per Serving: Cal 464; Prot 4 g; Carbo 99 g; Fiber 1 g;
T Fat 7 g; 13% Calories from Fat; Chol 53 mg; Sod 128 mg.

Party Puffs

1 8-ounce can juice-pack
   crushed pineapple
3 ounces light cream cheese,
   softened

1 cup light whipped topping
1 5-ounce package Stella D'Oro
   Anginetti cookies

Drain pineapple partially. Beat cream cheese and whipped topping at low speed in mixer bowl for 1 minute. Stir in pineapple. Slice tops off cookies. Drop creamed filling by teaspoonfuls onto bottom halves of cookies; replace tops. Chill until serving time. Yield: 12 servings.

Approx Per Serving: Cal 96; Prot 1 g; Carbo 12 g; Fiber <1 g;
T Fat 5 g; 44% Calories from Fat; Chol 11 mg; Sod 105 mg.

Pumpkin Cheesecake Bars

1 cup all-purpose flour
1/3 cup packed light brown sugar
5 tablespoons margarine, softened
1/2 cup chopped pecans
8 ounces light cream cheese,
   softened

1/2 cup canned pumpkin
3/4 cup sugar
2 eggs, slightly beaten
1 1/2 teaspoons vanilla extract
1 1/2 teaspoons cinnamon
1 teaspoon allspice

Preheat oven to 350 degrees. Mix flour and brown sugar in bowl. Cut in margarine until crumbly. Stir in pecans. Reserve 3/4 mixture. Press remaining mixture into 8x8-inch baking pan. Bake for 15 minutes. Cool. Combine remaining ingredients in mixer bowl. Beat at medium speed until smooth. Pour over baked crust. Sprinkle with reserved crumb mixture. Bake for 30 to 35 minutes or until set. Cool on wire rack. Cut into bars. Yield: 15 servings.

Approx Per Serving: Cal 200; Prot 4 g; Carbo 25 g; Fiber 1 g;
T Fat 10 g; 44% Calories from Fat; Chol 37 mg; Sod 144 mg.

Beverages

Apple-Pineapple Punch

1 46-ounce can pineapple juice
1 12-ounce can frozen apple
   juice concentrate, thawed

1 12-ounce can frozen orange
   juice concentrate, thawed
3 1-liter bottles of diet ginger ale

Combine pineapple juice, apple juice concentrate and orange juice concentrate in freezer container; mix well. Freeze for 2 days. Place mixture in punch bowl. Add ginger ale 1 hour before serving. Yield: 20 servings.

Approx Per Serving: Cal 93; Prot 1 g; Carbo 23 g; Fiber <1 g;
   T Fat <1 g; 1% Calories from Fat; Chol 0 mg; Sod 19 mg.

Apple Spice Spritzer

2 12-ounce cans frozen apple
   juice concentrate, thawed
2 oranges, sliced
2 lemons, sliced

2 4-inch cinnamon sticks
2 whole cloves
5 cups club soda, chilled

Combine apple juice concentrate, fruit and spices in saucepan. Bring to a boil; reduce heat. Simmer, covered, for 15 minutes; strain juice into pitcher. Chill in refrigerator. Add club soda just before serving. Yield: 8 servings.

Approx Per Serving: Cal 161; Prot 1 g; Carbo 40 g; Fiber 1 g;
   T Fat <1 g; 2% Calories from Fat; Chol 0 mg; Sod 53 mg.

Mock Champagne

1 cup sugar
1 cup water
2¹/₄ cups grapefruit juice
1 cup orange juice
³/₄ cup grenadine syrup
3 quarts diet ginger ale

Combine sugar and water in saucepan. Bring to a boil, stirring frequently. Remove from heat. Cool slightly. Add juices and grenadine syrup; mix well. Chill until serving time. Add ginger ale just before serving. Yield: 16 servings.

Approx Per Serving: Cal 119; Prot <1 g; Carbo 23 g; Fiber <1 g; T Fat <1 g; 1% Calories from Fat; Chol 0 mg; Sod 18 mg.

Hot Cranberry Cider

6 cups apple cider
4 cups cranberry juice
¹/₃ cup packed light brown sugar
Peel of ¹/₂ lemon
3 cinnamon sticks
¹/₄ teaspoon cloves

Combine apple cider, cranberry juice, brown sugar, lemon peel, cinnamon sticks and cloves in saucepan; mix well. Simmer for 30 minutes. Remove cinnamon sticks. Pour into cups. Yield: 12 servings.

Approx Per Serving: Cal 135; Prot <1 g; Carbo 34 g; Fiber <1 g; T Fat <1 g; 1% Calories from Fat; Chol 0 mg; Sod 9 mg.

Instant Boiled Custard

2 4-ounce packages vanilla
   instant pudding mix
8 cups low-fat milk
1 teaspoon vanilla extract
1 15-ounce can sweetened
   condensed milk

Combine pudding mix and milk in mixer bowl; mix well. Add vanilla and condensed milk; beat until smooth. Yield: 10 servings.

Approx Per Serving: Cal 317; Prot 10 g; Carbo 54 g; Fiber <1 g; T Fat 8 g; 21% Calories from Fat; Chol 32 mg; Sod 303 mg.

At parties, set up the drink station away from the food to avoid overcrowding.

Fruit Punch

1/2 cup sugar
1/2 cup water
12 whole cloves
2 2-inch cinnamon sticks

3 6-ounce cans frozen orange
    juice concentrate, thawed
1 quart apple juice

Bring sugar, water, cloves and cinnamon sticks to a boil in saucepan; reduce heat. Simmer for 10 minutes. Strain into large pitcher. Prepare orange juice concentrate using package directions. Add orange juice and apple juice to sugar mixture; mix well. Chill until serving time. Yield: 8 servings.

Approx Per Serving: Cal 208; Prot 2 g; Carbo 51 g; Fiber 1 g;
     T Fat <1 g; 1% Calories from Fat; Chol 0 mg; Sod 6 mg.

Golden Glow Punch

3 cups grapefruit juice
1 cup tangerine juice
1/2 cup light corn syrup

2 cups chilled seltzer water
1 grapefruit, peeled, sliced
1 cup sliced strawberries

Blend grapefruit juice, tangerine juice and corn syrup in pitcher. Chill, covered, until serving time. Pour over ice cubes in small punch bowl. Add seltzer water; mix gently. Garnish with grapefruit and strawberry slices. Yield: 8 servings.

Approx Per Serving: Cal 145; Prot 1 g; Carbo 37 g; Fiber 2 g;
     T Fat <1 g; 2% Calories from Fat; Chol 0 mg; Sod 12 mg.

Kiwi-Yogurt Smoothie

2 kiwifruit, sliced
1 banana
1/4 cup plain low-fat yogurt

3 ice cubes
2 large strawberries

Combine kiwifruit, banana, yogurt and ice cubes in blender container. Process until puréed. Pour into 2 glasses. Garnish with strawberries. Yield: 2 servings.

Approx Per Serving: Cal 122; Prot 3 g; Carbo 28 g; Fiber 4 g;
     T Fat 1 g; 8% Calories from Fat; Chol 2 mg; Sod 25 mg.

Index